Literature in Perspective

Reading is a pleasure; reading great literature is a great pleasure, which can be enhanced by increased understanding, both of the actual words on the page and of the background to those words, supplied by a study of the author's life and circumstances. Criticism should try to foster understanding in both aspects.

Unfortunately for the intelligent layman and young reader alike, recent years have seen critics of literature (particularly academic ones) exploring slender ramifications of meaning, exposing successive levels of association and reference, and multiplying the types of ambiguity unto seventy times seven.

But a poet is 'a man speaking to men', and the critic should direct his efforts to explaining not only what the poet says, but also what sort of man the poet is. It is our belief that it is impossible to do the first without doing the second.

Literature in Perspective, therefore, aims at giving a straightforward account of literature and of writers—straightforward both in content and in language. Critical jargon is as far as possible avoided; any terms that must be used are explained simply; and the constant preoccupation of the authors of the Series is to be lucid.

It is our hope that each book will be easily understood, that it will adequately describe its subject without pretentiousness so that the intelligent reader who wants to know about Donne or Keats or Shakespeare will find enough in it to bring him up to date on critical estimates.

Even those who are well read, we believe, can benefit from a lucid expression of what they may have taken for granted, and perhaps—dare it be said?—not fully understood.

K. H. G.

Chronological List of Dickens's Principal Works

1836 *Sketches by Boz*
1837 *The Posthumous Papers of the Pickwick Club*
     The Strange Gentleman (play)
1838 *Oliver Twist*
     Nicholas Nickleby
     The Memoirs of George Grimaldi
     Sketches of Young Gentlemen
1840 *Sketches of Young Couples*
1841 *Master Humphrey's Clock* (including *The Old Curiosity Shop*
     and *Barnaby Rudge*)
1842 *American Notes*
1843 *A Christmas Carol*
1844 *Martin Chuzzlewit*
     The Chimes
1845 *The Cricket on the Hearth*
1846 *Pictures from Italy*
1847 *The Haunted Man*
1848 *Dombey and Son*
1850 *David Copperfield*
1852 *Bleak House*
     A Child's History of England
     Stories for Christmas
1854 *Hard Times*
1855 *Little Dorrit*
1856 *The Frozen Deep* (play with Wilkie Collins)
1858 *A House to Let*
1859 *A Tale of Two Cities*
     The Haunted House
1860 *The Uncommercial Traveller*
1861 *Great Expectations*
1863 *Mrs. Lirriper's Lodgings*
1865 *Dr. Marigold's Prescriptions*
     Our Mutual Friend
1870 *The Mystery of Edwin Drood* (unfinished)

Literature in Perspective
General Editor: Kenneth Grose

Dickens

A. H. Gomme

Evans

Evans Brothers Limited London

Published by Evans Brothers Limited
Montague House, Russell Square, London, W.C.1

First published 1971

To Susan

Set in 11 on 12 point Bembo and printed in Great Britain
by the Camelot Press Ltd., London and Southampton
237 35014 9 cased
237 35015 7 limp

PRA 2702

Dickens

Of the making of books there is no end. This century has been particularly prolific in the making of books about books, and it may seem hard to justify yet another addition to the vast amount of reading matter that now surrounds Dickens. Yet with so inexhaustible a writer, there will perhaps always be room for a fresh individual report. The changes in Dickens's reputation during the century and a third since *Pickwick*—more especially the changes in the relative valuation of his various novels—must be enough to deter any but the most confident or most foolhardy from attempting a definitive judgment. Indeed it is hard, if my experience is at all typical, even to arrive at a settled decision about one's own views: I have found my own estimates of some of the novels changing substantially more than once; and the job of trying to become clear in writing about what one thinks, sometimes leads to the discovery that one thinks something different from what one had supposed. Naturally for the moment I believe I am about right in most of the views outlined in this little book, but I am aware enough of the past to expect to have sometimes to shift my ground in the future.

The great thing is to read Dickens with as much alertness and intelligence as possible, not just as a historical curiosity (though he has been for so many a chief source of knowledge about Victorian England), but as a novelist whose work is a constant stimulus to richer living now. As Edward Burne-Jones once said in answer to the remark that people have read Dickens's novels too much, 'No, they haven't read them too much, but they hurry through them and don't see how good they are.' So I hope I have at least managed to disturb a few too easily settled opinions and to encourage the thoughtful and thorough reading which Dickens at his splendid best repays with such rich and varied enjoyment.

I should like here to acknowledge, however inadequately, the great amount I have learnt from my wife about how to read Dickens, and the help I have received in preparing this book from discussion with Mrs. Dorothy Woolley, Mr. Francis Doherty, Mr. John Fry, Mr. Fred Inglis and Mr. David Rothwell. I also owe a great debt of thanks to Mr. Kenneth Grose for his patience, tolerant good humour and shrewdness in dealing with a very awkward author.

A. H. G.

Note: the following abbreviations have been used in references throughout the book: BH: *Bleak House*; BR: *Barnaby Rudge*; DC: *David Copperfield*; D & S: *Dombey and Son*; ED: *Edwin Drood*; GE: *Great Expectations*; HT: *Hard Times*; LD: *Little Dorrit*; MC: *Martin Chuzzlewit*; NN: *Nicholas Nickleby*; OCS: *Old Curiosity Shop*; OMF: *Our Mutual Friend*; OT: *Oliver Twist*; PP: *Pickwick Papers*; T2C: *A Tale of Two Cities*.

A Note by the General Editor

The object of the *Literature in Perspective* series is to give an up-to-date view of the main writers in English literature. Opinions change with changing times; one generation can see in a writer facets that were not readily apparent to his contemporaries. Only the greatest writers can hope to survive far beyond the days when what they were saying was 'relevant'. Hence it is common for a popular writer's stock to depreciate rapidly in the years immediately following his death, and the majority of them sink to be lost for ever.

DICKENS, popular in his own lifetime, has never lost his appeal to ordinary readers during the century that has passed since he died. But it is not until fairly recent years that he has gained the approval of academic critics. Indeed, it may fairly be said that the acclamation of millions of ordinary middle-brow readers has in some degree deterred serious critics from giving him their full attention. Up to the time of the Second World War, Dickens was the caricaturist who gave us Mrs. Gamp, Sam Weller, Mr. Squeers, Uriah Heep, Micawber; he was the social reformer who attacked workhouses, Yorkshire Do-the-boys Halls, London insanitary slums; and he was (with the help of the Prince Consort) the creator of Christmas. The works that people read were those that fostered this view of him: *Pickwick Papers, Oliver Twist, Nicholas Nickleby, A Christmas Carol, David Copperfield,* and, oddly enough, *A Tale of Two Cities.* It will be noticed from the chronological list of Dickens's main works, printed above, that these are, with one exception, among his earliest, coming before about 1850; the exception is a historical novel that is pretty bad history and pretty corny fiction. It was generally thought that

Dickens was a superb tear-jerking and laughter-provoking entertainer who happened to be a moralist, a sort of lay parson—a typical comment is: 'His morality is summed up in a general appeal to goodness, generosity and loving-kindness.'

But as the century drew to its close, a new generation of literary critics (foremost among whom was perhaps Edmund Wilson) turned with fresh unprejudiced eyes to Dickens. The result was that he was seen to have a tragic rather than a comic view of life, a profound sense of the tears in things. In struggling to give expression to his gloomy vision he created huge symbols that move like Wordsworthian 'forms' through the novels of his maturity: the prison in *Little Dorrit*, the fog in *Bleak House*, the dust heap (less evocative perhaps) in *Our Mutual Friend*, the cobwebbed shell of a wedding-cake (less pervasive perhaps) in *Great Expectations*. The novels that seemed now to be the most powerful were those that came after 1850, though these were foreshadowed by *Dombey and Son* (1847–8), where he 'achieved a form by means of which he could convey the more detailed and philosophic social criticism that was to animate his work in the future'—to quote a modern critic.

Thus any book of the shortness of this one which would aim at presenting an up-to-date perspective of this prolific author must necessarily concentrate on the later works, if it was not to become a mere *catalogue raisonné*, with natty little synopses and smart references to Dickens's brilliance in character-sketching and his reforming zeal. This would have been to belittle Dickens, who is now seen in some circles to be the greatest English poet since Shakespeare. It is hoped that this short book will reveal him as the profound philosophical observer of life, and the great creative artist, that he is.

K. H. G.

Contents

The Author

A. H. Gomme, M.A., Ph.D., is Senior Lecturer in English at the University of Keele.

Acknowledgments

The authors and the publishers are indebted to the following for permission to use illustrations: The British Museum for photographs of the cover of the first monthly number of *Little Dorrit*, the picture of Snow's Rents, Westminster, Phiz's illustration from *David Copperfield* and the View of a Dust Yard, and Dickens House for the cover photograph.

I

Dickens's Life

For most readers Dickens is so closely associated with Victorian England that a reminder may occasionally be necessary that he was already twenty-five and had lived more than two fifths of his life before Victoria came to the throne. Almost all his creative writing, virtually everything by which he is now known, does indeed come afterwards; but his early years were enormously influential on his career as a writer, and he was constantly preoccupied with the particular experiences of his youth and with the social conditions of the world in which he grew up. Dickens was thus in many ways an archetypal early Victorian (when he died nearly half of Victoria's long reign was still to come)—growing up, like the age he has come to represent, in the aftermath of a protracted and impoverishing war, when the colossal human and social problems of the industrial revolution were becoming inescapably apparent to all, sharing in and expressing with the sharpened perception of an artist the mixture of euphoric optimism and chronic depression which characterised so much of the middle years of the century. In his mature novels Dickens's optimism, what there is of it, is always personal or private, dwelling on what can be achieved through individual love and benevolence: when he looks at the public world, the view is always of corruption, muddle and incompetence, and the novels ignore or dismiss the great collective movements towards social amelioration. For Dickens's working life spanned the first great period of social legislation in England, from the Factory Act and the New Poor Law of 1833 and 1834 to the Elementary Education Act of 1870. During this period major reforms were made in mines, factories and the conditions of labour, the trade unions, local and national government, public health, housing, education and the law. None of these could have been achieved without the concerted or centralised movements which Dickens in his novels seems to have no hopes of. But if Dickens's heroes have with some justice been accused of having benevolence but no policy, this is not true, or only partially so, of Dickens himself. This book is concerned with Dickens the novelist; but to gain a fair impression of Dickens as a social reformer one must read also his journalism (chiefly in his own periodicals, *Household Words* and *All the Year Round*) and his speeches.

Dickens was born on 7 February 1812 in a small but genteel house in Landport, a part of Portsmouth close to the dockyards, where his father, John Dickens, was a clerk in the Navy Pay Office. (The house, now 393 Commercial Road, still exists as a Dickens museum.) Charles was the second of eight children: the eldest was his sister Fanny (born 1810), to whom he was devoted, though as a boy sometimes jealous of the special treatment she seemed to receive at his expense. Dickens's father was Mr. Micawber, and his mother was Mrs. Nickleby. There is every reason to believe that these two fictional portraits represent very closely Dickens's view of his parents. The same kind of affectionate exasperation with which David Copperfield looks on Mr. Micawber can be seen in Dickens's attitude towards his father, who had all Mr. Micawber's fecklessness and charm and as frequently got into debts from which his son and others as regularly extracted him, though he never showed the qualities which led to Mr. Micawber's unexpected apotheosis as an efficient colonial magistrate. In fact Dickens's admiration for his father grew throughout his life; on the other hand he seems to have been fairly cold-blooded about his intentions in creating Mrs. Nickleby. It is said that Mrs. Dickens, on reading the novel, could not believe that anyone so silly could exist.

Within a few months of Charles's birth, John Dickens's prodigality led to a move to a poorer house; two years later he was transferred to London, and in 1816 to Chatham, where they lived (chiefly in Ordnance Terrace) for six years, which left an exceptionally keen impression on the boy's imagination and memory. The Medway towns and their surrounding area were made the setting of large sections of several novels, *Pickwick, Oliver Twist, Great Expectations* and *Edwin Drood,* with an episode in *David Copperfield.* (Bleak House was also originally intended to be near Rochester rather than St. Albans.) In his fiction they are by no means idealised, but north Kent remained something of a land of heart's desire for Dickens himself until finally he was able to buy the house at Gadshill, which became a mark of romantic ambition as soon as John Dickens pointed it out to the boy on a walk and remarked that one day he might live in it. Apart from gaining a close knowledge of the towns, Dickens had many experiences in Chatham which so absorbed his imagination that they coloured all the rest of his emotional life: it is hardly an exaggeration to say that most of the most intense feelings in his novels come from a habit of constantly reliving the experience of his childhood and youth. At Chatham he listened to the wild and terrifying stories of Mary Weller, the nursemaid, which he retells in *The Uncommercial Traveller*; here he first went to school, with a vinegary old woman who later became Mrs. Pipchin; here he saw convicts working in the dockyard and being marched back to the hulks; and here he was first introduced to the delightful world of the theatre and to the detestable world of little Bethels. His uncle took him to the Theatre Royal and his parents (who were fairly casual about religion) to the Zion Baptist Chapel, where the minister, William Giles, became the model for all the hypocritical dissenting clergymen of the novels, where the congregation was full of Mrs. Clennams, Mrs. Vardens and the Murdstones, and the services led him to permanently associate non-conformist religious practice with selfishness, meanness and spite. Giles, however, had a much more amiable and better-educated son, who kept a school at which Dickens, after leaving the dame school, was very happy, and who much encouraged his reading which had begun in earnest with a small library (mainly of 18th-century novels) kept, though apparently not read, by his father—books which were later to be the largest single influence on Dickens's own early stories.

In 1822 John Dickens was transferred to Somerset House and

the family moved back to London, where, owing to the again precarious financial position, they took a small house in a shabby half-built area of Camden Town, which at that time had a pretence of the gentility which the elder Dickens found so important. No thought seemed to be given at this time to any further schooling for Charles, who in consequence spent much time wandering in London—experience which tells in book after book. His godfather Christopher Huffam lived in Limehouse, which Dickens got to know intimately (see *Dombey and Son, Great Expectations* and *Our Mutual Friend*). By the end of the year John Dickens's cheerful carelessness had landed the family in such difficulties that Mrs. Dickens tried to start an educational establishment, with a brass plate, in Gower Street—to which, as to Mrs. Wilfer's, nobody came. There was then nothing for it but to pawn the furniture and the even more precious books: Charles was given the job and found his way into another new world. But worse came for him directly afterwards; James Lamert, a distant connexion of the family, had become manager of a blacking warehouse on the Thames waterfront on the site of the present Charing Cross station, an offshoot of the once famous 'Warren's Blacking'. Lamert offered Charles a job sticking labels on to bottles at six shillings a week for a twelve-hour day—more than some other boys of his age were getting. His parents readily—much too readily, as Dickens felt—accepted the offer, which would mean that the child could almost pay for his own keep; and Charles went to work at the warehouse, where he stayed for six months, though later it appeared to him much longer. These six months were the most powerful experience of his life. 'No words can express the secret agony of my soul as I sunk into this companionship'—of rough cockney boys who, though friendly enough after a time, represented to him the end of all his hopes of 'growing up to be a learned and distinguished man'. So ashamed and humiliated was he by the work and the whole situation in which he found himself that he never afterwards talked of it to anyone. He did in fact write two descriptions of it—in *David Copperfield* (where the blacking is altered to wines and spirits) and in an autobiographical fragment which he could not bring himself to publish, so that his children first knew of this period after their father's death when the fragment was included in Forster's *Life*. Soon after Dickens started at the warehouse his father was at last arrested for debt and imprisoned in the Marshalsea, most of the family going with him, though Charles had lodgings outside and went to prison for his breakfast. Though John Dickens did not stay long in prison, a timely legacy coming to release him in 1824, his son never completely escaped its influence. There is hardly a novel in which prisons or the fear of prison do not play some part, and *Little Dorrit* is dominated by them. In later life he made a point of visiting the prison in each new town he went to. The marked vein of pessimism so plain in the mature novels is certainly in large part the outcome of the ugliness of these episodes of his childhood—horror of a world in which such things can happen. And the almost manic exuberance to which comedy sometimes extends is its obverse, an attempt to forget the horror in extravagant fun.

The job in the blacking warehouse did not end immediately on John Dickens's release, but almost by accident a little later when his father saw him displayed at work in a front window, quarrelled with Lamert and took the boy away. Mrs. Dickens was for making up the quarrel and sending Charles back, for which he never afterwards forgave her. But he did not go back and was once again sent to school—in an academy off the Hampstead Road near Euston, which appears as Mr. Creakle's school in *David Copperfield,* though in fact Dickens was a good deal less unhappy there than David. He stayed three years, and then, in 1827 when he was fifteen and the family again in trouble, he went to work in a solicitor's office in Gray's Inn—his first connexion with the law, which likewise became something of an obsessive presence in the novels. Here, having to take messages to many legal offices, he first made acquaintance with various branches of the Circumlocution Office. But he now had time and money to go back to his favourite enjoyment of the theatre, not only as a spectator, but also as an actor himself in the private theatres where one could pay a fairly stiff price for the privilege of taking part. There is a vast deal of the theatre in Dickens: in addition to the handful of (very lightweight) plays and to such things as the Crummles section of *Nicholas Nickleby* and Wopsle (alias Waldengarver) in *Great Expectations,* all the great 'scenes' in Dickens's novels—the dramatic encounters and revelations to which the rest seems often no more than a preparation—are conceived as pieces of theatre in which one is all the time conscious of the actor's voice. The two greatest theatrical influences on Dickens were the tragedian W. C. Macready, who later became a close friend and on whom Dickens modelled his own acting, and Charles Mathews, whose presentations sometimes included playlets in which he played all the parts, which he helped the audience to identify by giving them tag-lines, a trick which Dickens often copied, though in a novel it has not the same function and is often tiresome.

He had no intention of spending the rest of his life in a solicitor's office, with its boredom and slow rise in salary, and so used much of his spare time learning shorthand in order to equip himself as a journalist. By 1829 he was confident enough of his powers to leave one branch of the law and enter another, as freelance reporter in the police courts and Doctors' Commons, episodes which have left their mark in *Oliver Twist* and *David Copperfield.* He seems to have liked this life little better than the other, having to depend for work on lawyers whose faces 'bespoke nothing but conceit and silliness'; and for a time he had serious thoughts of the stage as a career and got as far as fixing an appointment with Charles Kemble, which (providentially) he was unable to keep. The next three years were dominated by his passion for Maria Beadnell and his attempts to persuade both her and her parents to accept him as a suitable match. She was the attractive, but flirtatious and silly, daughter of a banker, and she played with him for a long time before letting him drop. Her portrait as a young woman appears first as Dolly Varden in *Barnaby Rudge* and then more fully as the spoiled and artless Dora Spenlow (*David Copperfield*). Twenty years later, at the height of the distress caused by his unfortunate marriage, Dickens met her again: he had eagerly looked forward to the meeting, but in the event it shocked him profoundly. She 'who had been spoiled and artless long ago was determined to be spoiled and artless now'. So Dora became Flora Finching in *Little Dorrit,* and Arthur Clennam relives his author's disillusion, as much in vengeance on his old captivation as in anguish at the change (or lack of it) in the woman to whom he had once so painfully exposed himself.

In 1831 Dickens was offered a job as reporter on the *Mirror of Parliament,* a periodical lately started by his uncle J. H. Barrow and consisting, like *Hansard,* of verbatim parliamentary reports. John Dickens, who had retired from the Navy Office in 1827 and had likewise learnt shorthand, was already on the staff. Charles immediately proved to be an outstanding reporter and was able to add reporting for the *True Sun* to his work for the *Mirror.* He remained a parliamentary reporter for five years, most of the time for the influential liberal paper the *Morning Chronicle,* to which he moved in 1833. He thus first came into close contact with parliamentary affairs at the time of the debates on the Reform Act (Grey's first reform bill was thrown out in 1831), which led to a substantial change in the character of the membership of the House of Commons. From 1832 onwards there were a good many members who were strongly influenced by the views of the Utilitarian, Jeremy Bentham, and the philosophic radicals, and Dickens imbibed much which finds later expression in his speeches and journalism written in support of radical reform measures. At the same time, however, he learnt a contempt for Parliament and parliamentary procedure which never left him. Parliament remained for him the prime example of 'how not to do it', a monument of inefficiency and graft. Despite the Reform Act, Parliament still seemed to be run by the Coodles and Doodles, the Buffeys and Duffeys, the old families between whom it was impossible to distinguish any essential difference; and the new men were the Merdles and Veneerings who bought their way in and never acted from disinterested principle. Dickens's collective term for Parliament was the national dustheap—a word whose true significance for the 19th century is half-hidden from us: dust was a euphemism for the piles of ashes, decaying filth and human excrement which were all too familiar a feature of the streets of London and other large cities.

Obviously Dickens's generalisations are misleading and unfair; and a comparison with Disraeli's *Sybil,* for example, shows his distance from a writer who really knew the workings of Parliament from the inside. Yet Disraeli's political satire is no less acid than Dickens's. And it is a somewhat chastening reminder of the slow effect of change that of the seven men who were Prime Minister between the Reform Acts of 1832 and 1867, only two—Peel and Russell—were at the time in the Commons, and Russell was himself a member of an ancient landed family.

These years were also full of wanderings through London, especially at night after Dickens had finished transcribing his notes. His habit of close observation of people at work provided him not only with the material of his earliest sketches, but also with the intimate knowledge of the common life of London streets which makes the staple background of all the novels. What he saw especially was people at their jobs: a man's job became part of his character, frequently defining it—it is impossible to imagine Mrs. Gamp or Mr. Snagsby changing their jobs. Dickens's first sketch, written in imitation of a current fashion, was offered to the *Monthly Magazine,* where it was published in December 1833. The editor wanted more, Dickens obliged, and though the magazine had only a small circulation, the sketches quickly became known. In August 1834 he started using the pseudonym Boz; soon afterwards the *Chronicle* began printing his work and paying for it: he was now earning seven guineas a week. For a man in his early twenties, this was good money, and Dickens began to appear as something of a dandy, a character in which he reappears in *David Copperfield* and which also perhaps inspired Mr. Toots. But he had constantly to support his father whose creditors were always threatening; and the offer by the publisher Macrone of £150 for the copyright of the first edition of the *Sketches* in book form could not be refused. It came out in 1836.

In 1834 Dickens had taken rooms for himself and his brother Fred in Furnival's Inn, Holborn. At about this time he became intimate with the family of George Hogarth, editor of the *Evening Chronicle*. There were six sons and eight daughters, and

Dickens duly fell in love with the eldest girl, Catherine, to whom he was engaged in 1835 and married the next year. In fact he seems rather to have fallen in love with all the daughters collectively. To the second, Mary, who came to live with the Dickenses in Holborn soon after their marriage, he was particularly devoted. She died suddenly in 1837 at the age of eighteen; and Dickens never completely got over the profound shock. He repeatedly idealised her in the suffering innocent girls who are so familiar a feature of his novels from *Oliver Twist* onwards: Rose Maylie, Little Nell, Kate Nickleby, Mary Graham, Florence Dombey, Agnes Wickfield, Esther Summerson, Ada Clare, Sissie Jupe, Little Dorrit and Lizzie Hexam all bear witness to Dickens's love for Mary Hogarth.

In December 1835 Chapman and Hall approached Dickens to write the letterpress for a series of humorous sporting sketches to be drawn by the popular artist Robert Seymour. Dickens proposed that the theme be changed to that of a club of eccentric peripatetics; and he, rather than Seymour, became the leading partner. The monthly parts in which the Pickwick series was published were not at all a popular success until the introduction of Sam Weller in the fifth number; and before this Seymour, whose mental health had long been precarious, shot himself. It was imperative to find another illustrator immediately: Cruickshank was too busy; some, including Thackeray, were tried and found unsatisfactory; eventually Hablot Knight Browne (who soon came to call himself Phiz) was chosen, and so began an almost lifelong association with Dickens. *Pickwick* soon became immensely popular, the sales rising to 40,000 copies per month. When the story came to an end in 1837, it was worth several publishers' while to get other writers to produce inferior imitations and continuations, so much had Pickwick become a household word.

By the time of the publication of *The Pickwick Papers* as a book, when he was still only twenty-five, Dickens had become something of a *grand homme,* expansive, extravagant and rash. His letters at this time are particularly racy and vigorous. He took on several big commitments with different publishers, not all of which he was able to fulfil. A tempting offer from Richard Bentley, which Dickens managed to improve, started him off on *Oliver Twist,* which was begun before *Pickwick* was finished and likewise published in monthly parts—in *Bentley's Miscellany,* of which Dickens was himself the first editor. This clashed with a previous contract with Macrone, with whom he now quarrelled and from whom he eventually bought himself free at great expense. At the same time he agreed with Bentley to write a 'successor' to *Pickwick,* another novel (*Barnaby Rudge,* originally promised to Macrone as *Gabriel Varden, the Locksmith of London*), and to edit the memoirs of Grimaldi, the famous clown. As if this were not enough, before the end of 1838 he had embarked on *Nicholas Nickleby* for Chapman and Hall. This had a much larger sale even than *Pickwick* and led Dickens to put a higher financial value on his work than his contract with Bentley allowed for. He forced Bentley to raise the payments he had already agreed, but in the end came to have such a horror of him that he left him altogether, again at large cost to himself, and returned to Chapman and Hall, but as his own master. With them he began to edit a weekly periodical, *Master Humphrey's Clock,* which ran from April 1840 to November 1841. At first it was to contain only sketches, essays and short stories; but by the fourth number public clamour was so strong that Dickens began a novel, whose parts thus came out weekly. This was *The Old Curiosity Shop*; when it was finished he immediately followed with *Barnaby Rudge. Master Humphrey's Clock* was a source of good profit to Chapman and Hall, but most of all to Dickens.

In all his difficulties with his publishers, in which his own part does not always appear very honourable, Dickens turned for help to John Forster, who was the trusted adviser of most of the foremost literary figures of the time. Dickens was often annoyed by Forster's stubbornness and caution, but their quarrels were never lengthy, and it was on Forster that Dickens above all leant. At this time he leant on him a good deal for personal reasons as well; for now, after the death of Mary Hogarth, he began to long to get away from the company of his wife. In January 1837 his eldest son was born and named after him twice over—Charles

Culliford Boz. (Apparently the Boz came in because Grand-father Dickens excitedly shouted it out at the christening. All Dickens's sons were named after eminent writers, whose Christian and surnames they bore together.) Charles was the first of a series of more or less annual babies, the responsibility for which Dickens illogically rested almost wholly on his wife. In truth, as the years of his marriage wore on, he came to realise more and more the extent of the distance between their characters and interests, and the births of his children appeared to him as the public reminder of an association with her of which he was ashamed. Meanwhile financially they prospered, moving first to 48 Doughty Street (now Dickens House), then to Devonshire Terrace, Regent's Park, and finally to Tavistock Square.

Politically and emotionally Dickens was a child of the 'thirties. Much in what he wrote at the time was extremely topical. The early pages of *Oliver Twist* stem from the widespread hatred and distrust of the operation of the new Poor Law, which were particularly intense during the severe winter of 1837–8. In fact Dickens applauded some of the measures introduced by the act of 1834, but the workhouse in *Oliver Twist* is one which, like many of the time, had inherited the incompetence and cruelty of the old law and added a greater severity in application. Certainly it was the aim of the reformers to make the diet sparse and the houses generally uncomfortable in order to encourage people to find outside work, and the thrift and self-help which became such well-known Victorian virtues and were impressed so firmly by the rich on the poor: the diet in *Oliver Twist* was not very much of a caricature. Again, *Barnaby Rudge,* which Dickens had found himself unable to write when he first agreed to do it, was in large part prompted by his fear of mob-violence which had been greatly stirred by the Birmingham riots of 1839 and the threat of revolution which continued to hang over the country. In *The Old Curiosity Shop* he had hamfistedly introduced a paragraph or two of anti-Chartist propaganda; in *Barnaby Rudge,* by casting the story at the time of the Gordon Riots in 1780 (which were sparked off by anti-Catholic feeling but expressed a much wider discontent), he was able to give an extra sense of reality to his scenes of devastating riot: this after all was something that had really happened.

In 1842 Dickens made his first visit to America. The crossing of the Atlantic was appalling and dangerous, even worse than that described in *Martin Chuzzlewit*. Despite a great popular welcome, he was, as he wrote to Macready, hugely disappointed: 'the more I think of its youth and strength, the poorer and more trifling in a thousand aspects it appears in my eyes'. The Press he found 'more mean, and paltry, and silly, and disgraceful than in any country I ever knew'; the democracy seemed to him largely a fraud, the manners of the country profoundly distasteful. He offended a good many Americans by his attitude to slavery, others by his insistence on tackling the vexed question of the copyright system from which he, like other English writers, suffered, gaining nothing from the American editions of his books. When he returned to England and began *Martin Chuzzlewit,* it is said that he sent Martin and Mark Tapley to America in the hopes that an adventure in the New World would boost the flagging sales at home. The device is artistically dubious, and the effect in the novel haphazard. Yet these scenes, which—to an Englishman at least!—are easily the most enjoyable in the book, plainly contain within themselves not only Dickens's own reaction to his trip as a whole, but much of the pain he felt at the rawness of an undeveloped civilization. The book may be said to represent the end of the first main phase of Dickens's career as a novelist. Up to this point the stories have been devised with none but an arbitrarily contrived coherence, sometimes being little more than casually linked chains of adventure and depending on the thread of mystery to hold them together. There is only the most rudimentary attempt at psychological portrayal (with the striking exception of the closing pages of *Oliver Twist* and occasional flashes in *Barnaby Rudge*); 'character' is invented essentially for its own sake and not for any true relation it may have to the overall pattern of the novel. From this point on, the novels have doubtless less ebullience, but they are far more carefully and coherently planned.

Martin Chuzzlewit was not a commercial success, and by 1843

Dickens's lavish housekeeping had run him into debt. The immediate outcome was the first of his Christmas books, *A Christmas Carol,* which also was a comparative failure (owing, Dickens thought, to the publishers' having priced it too high). This determined him to live abroad for a while and so save money and spite his publishers. So in 1844 he took his family to Marseilles and then to Genoa. Here he began the second Christmas book, *The Chimes,* but found he needed the inspiration of the London streets. His attitude to London was always ambivalent. Though his report on it was toned down by his self-censorship, he never closed his eyes to its disgraces—slums, crime, poverty, disease—from which the countryside represented a retreat into cleanliness and innocence. Yet most of his work until the last years was done in London, and it was there that he seems to have composed most easily. In 1845 he was back. Georgina Hogarth, Kate's much younger sister, now became a regular part of the Dickens family and stayed with him till his death. At the same time he began to take an active part in the Ragged School movement, part of a general increase in his social activity which coincided with his close friendship with the philanthropist Angela Burdett-Coutts, with whom he worked for many years.

In 1846 Dickens was for a short time editor of the new liberal *Daily News,* the paper which much later joined forces with his old friend the *Morning Chronicle* to make the *News Chronicle,* which survived until only a few years ago. He soon left England again—this time for Lausanne, where *Dombey and Son* was begun. It is a turning point. In previous novels Dickens has been concerned with certain social evils, but they have all been looked at in isolation, and his main preoccupation has been with personal meannesses—hypocrisy, cruelty, selfishness. Now for the first time it can be said that society as a whole becomes his subject. At this time the movement which culminated in the great Public Health Act of 1848 had gathered force. Disease, as he was to insist so particularly in *Bleak House,* knows no barriers of class, and the promotion of public health is an issue which therefore concerns all society. The *links* between classes in *Dombey and Son* are still somewhat forced, in the melodramatic details of the relationship between Edith and Alice Marwood. But in this novel, in which for the first time Dickens takes a preoccupation with class seriously (see further pp. 113–16), he has found a theme to give overall unity to the vast human landscape of his imaginative observation: it is no accident that it was also his first thoroughly contemporary novel, the details as well as the theme very much of the moment. (The bank crisis of 1847 may have concentrated Dickens's interest on the question of money, though the effects of public failure do not have the wide social effects they have in *Little Dorrit*.)

Dombey and Son is not a comfortable book, and it has little of the irrepressible exuberance of the earlier work, so full of the exultant self-recreating energy which takes delight simply in the multiplication of life. After finishing the book, Dickens needed a long rest at Broadstairs. But following a lean period, there was once again a big popular success, and this seems to have encouraged a great new spurt of creativity: four novels came in the seven years after *Dombey* was finished, together with the *Child's History of England* (a rather absurd potpourri of vehement and partisan judgments on history, with the Pope as the chief villain), short stories and a new weekly magazine, *Household Words*. The first of the novels was *David Copperfield* (1849–50). Ever afterward this was Dickens's favourite novel, and it is not hard to see why: David is the closest he came to writing a self-portrait (including an oblique description of the terrible months in the blacking warehouse); and in this novel he not only gave a romanticised version of his own life but created in the conclusion a vicarious fulfilment of the daydream of his love for Mary Hogarth, lovingly drawn out to tease the reader with soft sorrow before the final glow of happiness. In *David Copperfield* it is the silly *ingénue* Dora who dies, leaving David free in the end to marry the ideal woman in Agnes. As with most daydreams (which allow a 'realisation' of the impossible), the object of desire is transformed into an ideal counterpart to the dreamer's ideal conception of himself, and therefore cannot really be made available to the outside world. Agnes is probably Dickens's largest single miscalculation of the reader's response: even those who share his partiality for the novel find it hard to believe in her or to treat her to the same solemn worship as she receives from David and his creator. And indeed, so personally absorbed is Dickens in so many of the details and main episodes of the story that it is impossible for him to achieve the objectivity which is necessary for the making of art out of direct experience; this first large-scale use of the first person is significant—he was himself involved too closely in the events he relates for him to see that a coherent work of art could not be made out of such heterogeneous matter, and often the book reads like a none-too-well-conceived autobiography (as at times it pretends to be).

Household Words was started in March 1850 and contained in its first number a story (*Lizzie Leigh*) by Mrs. Gaskell, whose first novel, *Mary Barton*, Dickens much admired. (Later *Cranford* and *North and South* both came out serially in *Household Words*.) The sombre realism of her best work seems certainly to have influenced Dickens in his work of the 1850s, though she has less of his self-censoring reticence. At any rate the descriptions of Tom-all-Alone's and the brickfields in *Bleak House* (1852-3) are bleak indeed, with a bleakness which is new in Dickens: even the wretched Oliver Twist can get a sort of fun in Saffron Hill, but no fun is ever possible in Tom-all-Alone's. *Bleak House* picks up with renewed energy the assault on social evils which was largely absent from *David Copperfield*. The shocking delays in the Court of Chancery and the widespread anguish they caused are treated with great ferocity, though here, as throughout the novels, Dickens offers no alternative to the vast complex of evils other than the private benevolence of individuals. *Bleak House* still contains a good deal of slack in such things as the laboured story of George Rouncewell and the Bagnets: what is above all impressive about it is the sense of interconnectedness—not so much the improbable family and personal links as the common fate hanging over all—expressive of Dickens's growing consciousness of how such great webs of evil encompassed the whole of society (and so had to be met by a comprehensive social movement which his novels do not allow for).

The labour of working at the monthly parts of *Bleak House* was so great that Dickens seriously considered never publishing periodically again, and had not intended to work on another story for a year. But late in 1853 he found himself 'laid by the throat' by the theme of *Hard Times,* for which he made a visit to Preston to observe a cotton spinners' strike which had dragged on for weeks. He also visited Manchester and seems to have talked over the novel with Mrs. Gaskell. The strike was written up in *Household Words* in February 1854, and *Hard Times* itself came out in short weekly instalments—a restriction on the planning of the story which Dickens found 'CRUSHING'. However that may be, the effect has been a single-minded concentration and a poetic tautness and density of language unique in his work, which have helped to give it its current very high reputation. It is also the only Dickens novel which takes place wholly outside London; yet the sense of place is remarkably vivid, even though the local accent is incredible. The major theme of *Hard Times* indicates a sharp reaction to supposed Benthamite principles; but it is one of the book's peculiar triumphs to have realised the closeness with which the 'philosophy of facts' was linked to the 'rugged individualism' which made the amelioration of industrial conditions so slow and painful.

This wonderfully rich series of novels came to an end with *Little Dorrit,* which, again contrary to firm intentions, he began thinking about within weeks of finishing *Hard Times.* The chief social impulse was his sense of outrage at the incompetence or (as he saw it) deliberate malfunctioning of the central administrative departments of government—in a word, circumlocution. This had been a nagging preoccupation with Dickens for many years: the immediate occasion of this great outburst was provided by his friend Henry Layard's attempts at administrative reform and above all the ineptitude of the Aberdeen coalition government and the shocking lack of all organisation in the Crimean campaign of 1854–5. Also in 1854 there was a terrible cholera epidemic in which 20,000 people died. Disease of this kind plays no direct part in *Little Dorrit,* but Dickens with some justice blamed the outbreak on the government's lack of interest in ensuring decent housing conditions in the big cities. The social impulse of the novel was clearer under its original title, *Nobody's Fault*: when Dickens was planning it, the Circumlocution Office was intended to play a larger and more obviously central role (see p. 161). But Mr. Dorrit's continued incarceration, as well as Doyce's troubles with his inventions, is laid at the door of circumlocution, and the theme of social involvement in which no man is an island is prominent throughout. In *Little Dorrit,* more powerfully perhaps than in any other novel, Dickens binds his whole structure together by a single all-encompassing metaphor, something which one may see him working towards in *Bleak House* and which he re-used with great subtlety and delicacy in *Great Expectations,* and somewhat less convincingly in *Our Mutual Friend.* The unfamiliarity of such a device in fiction may have been responsible for the scant critical acclaim of the later novels during the 19th century, though each outdid the one before in popular esteem.

In 1854 Dickens bought Gadshill Place, near Rochester, the house of his childhood dreams, and gave up the last of his series of London homes. By the mid 'fifties, however, his relations with his wife, which had gradually deteriorated over a long period, had become intolerable to them both. The final break came over Dickens's relations with Ellen Ternan, a young actress who had taken part in one of the plays which he wrote as a relaxation from more serious work. Dickens's passion for her was plainly intensified by finding her unattainable, by his now maddened sense of his wife's inadequacies; and Kate Dickens, who had been extravagantly and unjustifiably jealous of many women, now had some cause, though there is no reason to believe that Ellen was Dickens's mistress before the separation: his reaction to his frustration had rather taken the form of exasperated escapades with Wilkie Collins or other friends; and it was eventually at Kate's insistence that a formal separation was arranged by Forster and Mark Lemon, the editor of *Punch.* At this time Dickens, according to his daughter Kate, 'behaved like a madman. This affair brought out all that was worst—all that was weakest in him. He did not care a damn what happened to any of us'. When Lemon refused to print a letter publicly exculpating Ellen Ternan, he quarrelled violently, not only with Lemon but with the proprietors of *Punch*, Bradbury and Evans, who were now also Dickens's own publishers.

This meant the end of *Household Words*. But it was soon succeeded by another weekly, *All the Year Round,* published by his old friends Chapman and Hall: it contained work by many prominent contemporary writers, including Charles Reade, Wilkie Collins and Charles Lever. The first number, which came out in April 1859, carried the first instalment of a new novel—*A Tale of Two Cities*. This was Dickens's second and last 'historical' novel in the sense that in it he deliberately turned to a period well in the past and dramatised well-known public events. It has long been one of his most widely read stories; yet though everyone relishes the vivid atmosphere of the opening or the heady scenes of the storming of the Bastille, there is little to be said for Dickens's account or use of the French Revolution. For the only time, perhaps, in his novels, Dickens falsifies a picture in the interest of a preconceived attitude: this was doubtless unconscious, but the fact remains that he has allowed his fear of violence and the power of the mob to blind him to the idealistic beginnings of the Revolution, so that its inspiration seems merely the lust for blood and power. Nor does the prison theme, continued from *Little Dorrit,* have anything like the inclusive power it has in the earlier book. The hero (or perhaps 'anti-hero') Sydney Carton represents a stage between Richard Carstone of *Bleak House* and Eugene Wrayburn of *Our Mutual Friend,* but Dickens seems to have little real human interest in him: he is, as Henry James would say, merely a figure, and the sense of wasted potential is given in no more than diagrammatic form; neither are his limitations and weaknesses anywhere seen in relation to the society which bred him. He is in fact, as the heroics of his self-sacrifice show, only the hero of a highly artificial melodrama.

The writing of *A Tale of Two Cities* had a strong restorative effect on Dickens's disturbed mental and emotional condition. The last decade of his life is a story of mounting overwork and feverish activity. (He said of himself, 'I am incapable of rest. I am quite confident that I should rust, break, and die, if I spared myself.') Nevertheless it began with what is perhaps his most perfectly achieved work of art, *Great Expectations,* in which he combines all the piquancy and directness of expression of a first-person narrative with remarkable honesty and objectivity of vision. Here we are no longer immediately concerned with society in the large, rather with a sense of how personal qualities eddy round the individual, affecting and interacting with those of others nearer or farther from him. *Great Expectations* is, in a wholly respectable sense, Dickens's most conventional novel: and it is also the one in which he shows in an admirably and un-expectedly quiet, unobtrusive way his keenest powers of psycho-logical penetration. Yet it is inescapably a Dickens novel: Pip's story is unimaginable, as Dickens tells it, without the framework of the fantastic fable of Magwitch and Miss Havisham and the worlds they create out of their misfortunes.

The last completed novel was *Our Mutual Friend,* finished in 1865. It is a reversion from *Great Expectations* to the social spaciousness of *Bleak House* and *Little Dorrit*: in fact it is Dickens's most conscious and deliberate study of society as a whole. The artistic whole that results is not to my mind altogether successful. In the recreation of the atmosphere of parts of London it is un-equalled. But Lizzie Hexam is painfully idealised: she is scarcely conceivable as her father's daughter, and from the start she is too obviously prepared for the happy outcome of the affair with Eugene Wrayburn, with the result that the moral point of their triumph over social convention is obscured. There is a further real and disquieting ambiguity in Bella's tale as well (see pp. 84–90). Yet there is a more varied range of technique and scene than in any of his previous work: its satire in particular is the keenest in all Dickens—the treatment of the Lammles, for example, does with splendid economy and force all that Thackeray achieves in the long wearisome stretches of *Vanity Fair.* On the other hand and in an entirely different manner, the growth of Bradley Headstone's fatal obsession, though it has been widely mis-understood, is described with notable understanding and un-compromising clarity.

The chief activity of the 1860s was, however, the great series of public readings from his works. Dickens's lifelong interest in the theatre and his talents as an actor, combined with the obviously theatrical character of so many scenes in the novels, might have set him off on this new career before 1858, when he first became a public entertainer. Probably the need for money was the immediate spur: he now had to pay for the upkeep of three establishments (for Ellen Ternan as well as for Mrs. Dickens, whom he allowed £600 a year), and the readings quickly proved financially very rewarding. At first they contained only comic scenes, taken largely from short stories and early work, especially *Pickwick*. In the second series, which lasted on and off from 1861 to 1863 and brought him apparently £190 a night, *David Copperfield* and *Nicholas Nickleby* were added. A third series, for which he wrote among others the sinister sketch *Doctor Marigold,* which became one of his favourite readings, occupied him between 1864 and 1867. During part of this time he became seriously ill. There is no doubt that the strain of the readings told heavily on him, but Dickens pooh-poohed the danger. By this time they had become an obsession—here he could at last meet his audience face to face. So when the prospect of an American tour in the winter of 1867-8 looked favourable he overrode all the objections of doctors and friends. The tour was a continuous triumph, enormously more enjoyable to Dickens than his first visit. When he returned to England (with a profit of over £20,000) he again became seriously ill, but nevertheless soon insisted on yet one more series of readings. For this last series (or perhaps for America) he added the murder of Nancy in *Oliver Twist*. The effect of this scene on audiences and on Dickens himself was overwhelming. His son reported fearful screaming when he was rehearsing in the garden; and on stage the scene took demonic possession of him. Faintings in the audience seem to have been frequent; and at the end he was always intensely excited, breathless and with a racing pulse. During the last five years of his life he was chronically nervous—partly as the result of his experiences in the disastrous train crash at Staplehurst, to which he refers in the postscript to *Our Mutual Friend*. In the end the readings (which did not finally stop until March 1870), after leaving him more than once on the edge of paralysis, destroyed him. He was only fifty-eight when he collapsed suddenly in June 1870, and died with *Edwin Drood* only partly written. He was buried in Westminster Abbey, and for three days the grave was kept open while a continuous stream of people came to pay final respects. He had attained a popularity in his lifetime unapproached by any other English author; and with some justice *The Times* said of him, 'Statesmen, men of science, philanthropists, the acknowledged benefactors of their race, might pass away and yet not leave the void which will be caused by the death of Charles Dickens.'

2

Techniques and Characteristics

(i) DICKENS AND THE ENGLISH LANGUAGE

F. R. Leavis's essay on *Hard Times* was first published as one of a series called 'The Novel as Dramatic Poem'. Clearly the word 'poem' is being used in a wider sense than the familiar one—wider even than when applied to a play of Shakespeare. But the point of using it is to insist that at its finest and most complete the novel has a unity, an interrelatedness and perhaps too a concentration on a single purpose, akin to those of a sonnet or an ode. Novels of course have characteristically a comprehensiveness that even the longest poems seldom attempt; the movement is slower and more expansive; there is more room to include more of life. Moreover if Henry James is right that the only excuse for the existence of a novel is that it does attempt to represent life, then copiousness, inclusiveness must be characteristic. Victorian novelists in particular were keen that the main actions of their books should be given the basis and context of a rich variety of observed life; and Dickens's enormous creative energy could hardly help issuing at times in extravagance and irrelevance. Several of his earliest works (*Pickwick Papers* and *Nicholas Nickleby* are the most obvious examples) have very little governing impulse from within and in consequence very little outward control, so that they become hardly more than anthologies of adventure, anecdote and experience more or less arbitrarily attached to certain figures who persist from beginning to end. In *Martin Chuzzlewit,* a much more coherent novel, Martin's experiences in America, by far the richest and most enjoyable part of the book, nevertheless can be argued to be a gigantic and almost accidental parenthesis. And even in the most completely successful works, so inexhaustible is Dickens's fancy that unpredictable shoots continually bud from the main stock. Consider Mr. F.'s Aunt in *Little Dorrit*: she really has no part to play in the development of any of the interwoven themes of the novel and seems only to be there for the fun of it. Yet her inexplicable presence adds to our sense of the quantity of life in Dickens's world, just as Flora's description of Mr. Finching's death gives a peculiar poetic lift, a sense of vividly, if oddly, particularised observation to ordinary experience:

> I will draw a veil over that dreamy life, Mr. F. was in good spirits his appetite was good he liked the cookery he considered the wine weak but palatable and all was well, we returned to the immediate neighbourhood of Number Thirty Little Gosling Street London Docks and settled down, ere we had yet fully detected the housemaid in selling the feathers out of the spare bed Gout flying upwards soared with Mr. F. to another sphere.   LD I, xxiv

The language here is an instance of the familiar and sometimes irritating Dickensian device, by which figures not quite at the centre of the story are given special tricks of speech, like badges by which they may be recognised, indicating normally a certain aspect of character which is then everlastingly fixed: Flora's breathless inconsequence remains to the end. Yet a whole way of life is momentarily recreated in this vignette; the real poetry of the little scene comes in the personification of Gout as an avenging angel that seems physically to collect and lift Mr. F. from the earth.

This is a tiny example of the characteristic resources of Dickens's language, of the delight he takes in exploiting language with the skill of a performing artist. The delight is not always the sign of the best art. In the railway journey in Chapter XX of *Dombey and Son* we find one of the most obvious cases of Dickens flexing his intellectual muscles in public. The effect—particularly in the insistent relation of the train and 'the remorseless monster Death'—is pretty blatant; yet within this somewhat vulgar display comes a remarkable evocation, depending on a subtle husbanding and manipulation of verbal rhythms, of the varied movement of the train over the rails—it can only be properly enjoyed when read aloud. It is in the resourcefulness and variety of his language that Dickens's power as a poet shows itself. But it is important to distinguish the truly creative language of Dickens from the superficially poetical, of which there is a great deal that is brought out regularly at moments when he himself is near to tears or intends to be especially solemn. Dickens is always ready with a solemn image for a solemn moment: so, Annie Strong, begging her husband's forgiveness, pleads:

> Oh, take me to your heart, my husband, for my love was founded on a rock, and it endures! DC xlv

Unfortunately the image here only makes the gesture, and hence the emotion appears stiff and unreal, for it is too obviously confected for the moment and its biblical association is unnatural and inappropriate. Again, Harriet, the self-sacrificing and uncomplaining sister of the errant but now repentant John Carker, is surrounded by a haze of would-be poetical language that does nothing beyond telling us that Dickens is feeling throbs of emotion about her:

> The cordial face she lifted up to his to kiss him was his home, his life, his universe, and yet it was a portion of his punishment and grief; for in the cloud he saw upon it—though serene and calm as any radiant cloud at sunset— . . . he saw the bitter fruits of his old crime, for ever ripe and fresh. D & S xxxiii

Note how the rhythm itself seems to pose, how commonplace, and how inert, the images are here—cordial, serene and calm, the radiant cloud at sunset—the mere stock-in-trade of cheap commemorative verse: no real woman is brought before us, just a notion of one; and the phrase which attaches itself to John Carker's crime—the bitter fruits—has, as one may see from the unfortunate 'ever ripe and fresh', in itself no element of thought and so no true feeling either: it is only there (irresistible as it must have been in such a mood) for its conventionally religious or religiose associations.

Dickens's true poetry does not lie in the loose emotional haze of stuff like this, nor yet in such curiosities as the passages in *Barnaby Rudge* and *The Old Curiosity Shop* which (without being printed as such) are essentially in blank verse: this is the Dickens who can never wholly escape from the theatre. Rather his poetry exists, in the first instance, in the quantities of vivid phrases which suddenly bring an item or a scene unforgettably to life, often with irrepressible humour. The Copperfields' maid has a cousin in the Life Guards 'with such long legs that he looked like the afternoon shadow of somebody else' (*DC,* xliv). Mr. Dombey, musing on his own magnificence, 'looked down into the cold depths of the dead sea of mahogany on which the fruit dishes and decanters lay at anchor' (*D & S,* xxx). How complete is the evocation here and in how few words! The dishes and decanters are *at anchor*—ships therefore at rest and in calm water, so that there are clear reflexions as in the polished mahogany, whose coldness and deadness seem to come from Mr. Dombey himself. And Mr. Dombey looked into the *depths*—not that he could literally see more than the surface of the wood, but that the reflexions, as at sea, implied depths, and it was hence 'as if the subjects of his thoughts were rising towards the surface one by one, and plunging down again'. (Note further how the ship-image just avoids being explicit, with a corresponding great increase in concentration: the decanters and mahogany are not simply *like* ships in harbour; for a moment they *are* ships in harbour.)

Sometimes images seem to bubble up just because Dickens's fancy is so continuously full of them:

> The little staircase windows looked in at the back windows of other houses as unwholesome as itself, with poles and lines thrust out of them, on which unsightly linen hung—as if the inhabitants were angling for clothes, and had had some wretched bites not worth attending to. LD I, ix

Is there more here than that Dickens has been struck by the ludicrous parallel between the appearance of the washing on poles and that of a fisherman's rod? Probably the angling image is not made closely relevant to Frederick Dorrit's observation; but in common with the other examples given and with so many others one could choose, it shows exactly what the Harriet Carker quotation does not—a writer with a very keen eye for fact, fully attentive and alert to detail and full of a need to convey the fact to the reader as vividly and accurately as possible. One further instance of this alertness—the pawnshop in *Dombey and Son* (Chapter ix), full of motionless clocks that 'seemed as incapable of being successfully wound up as the pecuniary affairs of their former owners'. Anyone tolerably awake to words might have noticed the oddity of the two such different uses of 'wound up'. No one but Dickens would have seized on it as the intimate connecting link between the melancholy motionless clocks and the sad state of affairs of which, lost and useless in the shop, they are the emblem.

Such imagistic and metaphorical writing has often a deeper or more sinister purpose. It may serve to record not merely a physical character but a moral or human one. Mr. Chadband, 'languidly folding up his chin into his fat smile' (*BH,* xix), is there before us not just as fat and well-fed, but as a complacent humbug. The horrible unnaturalness of the elderly Mrs. Skewton's parade of youthfulness provokes Dickens into an image of unmistakable, almost violent, bitterness, so that for a moment it is as if he has an intense personal hatred for his own creation:

> Flowers the maid was fastening on her youthful cuffs and frills, and performing a kind of private coronation ceremony on her, with a peach-coloured velvet bonnet; the artificial roses in which nodded to uncommon advantage, as the palsy trifled with them, like a breeze.
>
> D & S xxxvii

Note the exactness of the choice and placing of each word. For a moment there might be a *real* freshness in the scene, until we reach the monitory word 'artificial', the warning in which is even then momentarily allayed by the following phrase, which from being associated with youth and summer breezes is suddenly corrupted by the ugly reality, whose hideousness lies less in the thing itself than in the falsehood which attempts to pervert it into its opposite. Mrs. Skewton is always pretending to a youthfulness which she does not own—this in itself is an outward mark of her total emotional falseness—and here is her palsy, the sign of her decaying age, the very thing she makes a pretence of concealing, joining in the game of fraud. The whole horror of Mrs. Skewton's corruption is summarised and concentrated in half a sentence. This wonderful accuracy and economy of language occurs at times so unobtrusively that the reader may pass it unobserved. When her maid takes off the youthful dress, Mrs. Skewton 'tumbled into ruins like a house of painted cards' (*D & S*, xxx): not of course that painted cards collapse more completely than others—the adjective belongs to Mrs. Skewton, who is literally painted or made up, and hence in the old metaphor false: the word applied to the cards therefore brings them and her together into a yet tighter simile. The force of some of the most notable of these images is not always plain to the reader of today or even to Dickens's contemporaries. G. H. Ford (*Dickens and his Readers*, pp. 153f.) draws attention to the likening of Mrs. Podsnap in *Our Mutual Friend* to a rocking-horse, observing that she is 'presented to us as the driest of parties in a novel which has, as its central symbol, a dust-heap. A rocking-horse is filled with dusty stuffings, and its external lacquered rigidity is ideally appropriate to represent the artificiality of the person described'. G. H. Lewes certainly missed this, and so, probably, do many readers of Dickens today.

It is important to recognise that language, in Dickens as in Shakespeare, is the essential creative medium, itself an active part of the creative process. Often we can see the process going on in front of us. Veneering, making the conventional fatuous empty phrases that 'society' demands from speeches on celebratory occasions,

> is here to submit to you that the time has arrived when, with our hearts in our glasses, with tears in our eyes, with blessings on our lips, and in a general way with a profusion of gammon and spinach in our emotional larders . . . OMF xxxiii

Dickens's own deflationary phrases make a sandwich of the commonplaces of Veneering's speech. On a larger scale Pancks in *Little Dorrit* is first described as snorting and sniffing and puffing and blowing like 'a little labouring steam engine'; then a little later, Casby 'the Patriarch', his employer, is likened to an unwieldy ship in the Thames unable to make way by itself,

> when all of a sudden a little coaly steam-tug will bear down upon it, take it in tow, and bustle off with it; similarly the cumbrous Patriarch had been taken in tow by the snorting Pancks, and was now following in the wake of that dingy little craft.   LD I, xiii

It seems at first simply an example of the mercurial energy of Dickens suddenly alighting on an idea which flashes in front of us and is gone. Then, equally suddenly it is back, when Casby 'rose and went to the door by which Pancks had worked out, hailing that Tug by name. He received an answer from some little Dock beyond, and was towed out of sight directly.' The dock, which turns out to be Pancks's dingy office, confirms the image of the tug, which, still coaly and snorting and puffing, remains the mark of Pancks throughout the book: the image in fact creates and defines the whole character and position of Pancks. There are of course many phrases and images which, though momentarily striking, are much less fertile than this; yet so alive is Dickens to the possibilities of language that almost anything may become the occasion of a memorable crystallisation into words of the rapid flux of his perception.

Let us now look at a characteristic piece, not specially outstanding, of Dickens's atmospheric descriptive writing—from the opening of the third chapter of *Little Dorrit,* in which Arthur Clennam sees London for the first time for many years:

> It was a Sunday evening in London—gloomy, close, and stale. Maddening church bells of all degrees of dissonance, sharp and flat, cracked and clear, fast and slow, made the brick-and-mortar echoes hideous. Melancholy streets in a penitential garb of soot steeped the souls of the people who were condemned to look at them out of windows in dire despondency. In every thoroughfare, up almost every alley, and down almost every turning, some doleful bell was throbbing, jerking, tolling, as if the Plague were in the city and the dead-carts were going round. Everything was bolted and barred that could by possibility furnish relief to an overworked

people. . . . Nothing to see but streets, streets, streets. Nothing to breathe but streets, streets, streets. Nothing to change the brooding mind or raise it up. Nothing for the spent toiler to do but to compare the monotony of his seventh day with the monotony of his six days, think what a weary life he led, and make the best of it— or the worst, according to the probabilities.

No reader could miss the intention of this piece. The writing is rhetorical, self-assertive, using a number of simple literary devices—repetition, antithesis, personification, words heavy with emotional association. Dickens wishes not merely to describe the monotony of London but to recreate an experience of it in the reader: intentionally he keeps back the word 'monotony' till the last sentence of the paragraph, relying up to that point on the monotonous effect of his hammered-in appositive phrases— 'in *every* thoroughfare, up almost *every* alley, down almost *every* turning', 'throbbing, jerking, tolling'—till the dreariness is made plain and bleak at the end in the succession of crushing leaden sentences with no verb to bring them to life. Lest there should be any escape from this miserable scene, the streets themselves are represented as doing penance for their dismal state: 'a penitential garb of soot'—penitential first of all because soot is black and gloomy, but the word just hints at the sense, which will be so prominent later in the history of the Clennams, that there are crimes intimately connected with the city for which penance must be and is being done. There is an easy copiousness about the language, a sense of potential to be drawn upon, ranges and possibilities which will be opened up and explored.

Such a passage shows only one voice of Dickens: to get an impression of the range and flexibility of his poetic art one must experience the work at large, on a scale and in a detail which there is evidently no room for here. And as a matter of fact, the opening chapters of *Little Dorrit*, confident and completely competent as they are, depend for their effect on achieving a harsh concentration of attention on one object at a time, almost that is an *in*flexibility, so that the reader's mind remains firmly in front of the one thing Dickens wants him to see. In an excellent essay (*Dickens the Novelist*, pp. 1–29, especially pp. 2–5) Dr. Leavis has analysed something of the very different character of the opening of *Dombey and Son*: here I shall do no more than point to the perfectly controlled, though highly complex, presentation of the human scene we enter—a scene in which the principal moral conflict of the opposing claims of commercial grandeur and human tenderness is enriched by an astonishing variety of ironic and sympathetic observation. The flexibility of Dickens's art in these scenes is indeed wonderful: at the very start it seems, as we contemplate and enter into Dombey's satisfaction at having a son at last (to himself and to the firm), that we are firmly in the realm of sardonic comedy in which the contrast between the tiny vulnerability of the baby and the self-complacency of the father will be the occasion for irony alone. But the irony is interrupted and contradicted (as are Dombey's self-satisfied meditations) by the poignancy of Florence's direct expression of her need for and love of her mother, so complete a cipher in Dombey's world that she is looked on by him as a mere provider. The irony returns with a different, more grotesque note as the surgeon, confused by memories of his aristocratic patients, cannot recall who his present one is. Mrs. Chick, confident that all the poor dying Mrs. Dombey need do is to make an effort, and her friend Miss Tox, obsequiously deferential to the family grandeur, add further notes of irony, distancing us from the reality of the human scene, obliging us for the moment to look at it as in the frame which Dombey himself provides; yet the predominant effect remains one of pathos, to which the irony in fact ministers. The scene moves from the complacent unreality of Dombey's and Mrs. Chick's talk *about* the human situation with which in truth they are only notionally concerned, upstairs to the silence of Mrs. Dombey's room itself. Here Dickens brings us so sharply back to reality that even Mrs. Chick is for a moment baffled:

> There was such a solemn stillness round the bed; and the two medical attendants seemed to look on the impassive form with so much compassion and so little hope, that Mrs. Chick was for the moment diverted from her purpose. But presently summoning courage, and what she called presence of mind, she sat down by the

bedside,—and said, in the low, precise tone of one who endeavours to awaken a sleeper,

'Fanny! Fanny!'

There was no sound in answer but the loud ticking of Mr. Dombey's watch and Doctor Parker Pep's watch, which seemed in the silence to be running a race.

Dr. Leavis notes the sharp precision with which the 'peculiarly and impertinently insistent noise [of the watches] is evoked, giving us in immediacy the stillness of the death-chamber, and giving it as the fact and presence of death'. In the face of this reality, Mrs. Chick's self-important chatter can achieve nothing and only serves to highlight the contrast of the simple and unaffectedly human instinct of love by which Florence alone can kindle a last spark of life in her dying mother. And this points an overall irony, deeper than any before, that it is the disregarded Florence who has here (as she will have later) the power to arouse life and humanity, beyond anything that her father, with all his money, can do.

There is a different, rather less subtly varied presentation at the start of *Our Mutual Friend*. This is one of several occasions where Dickens uses a favourite trick of romantic fiction—of beginning with two chapters which narrate events which apparently have nothing to do with one another, whose juxtaposition is the start of a series of interlinked mysteries which make up the plot. The first chapter describes Lizzie Hexam and her father on the river: its function is above all to establish Lizzie as belonging to the river, but for a reason we as yet hardly guess at somehow detached from and shunning it. She pulls 'very easily' at the sculls, her every action is 'lithe', her father relies on her skill, and she responds instantly to every indication in his face. By a few light touches her intimacy with the river and its ways is established. Yet a deliberate mystery about their particular business is built up: none of the ordinary signs of a waterman's craft are present, and there is something disreputable about the appearance of the boat itself:

Allied to the bottom of the river rather than the surface, by reason of the slime and ooze with which it was covered, and its sodden state, this boat and the two figures in it obviously were doing something that they often did, and were seeking what they often sought.

As we fairly soon learn, they are indeed allied to the bottom of the river; and the man, though 'there was business-like usage in his steady gaze', showed half-savage: with his hook-nose and 'his bright eyes and his ruffled head, [he] bore a certain likeness to a roused bird of prey'.

So, though the reason for the 'touch of dread or horror' in the girl's look is as yet unexplained, there is that in the presentation of the scene to alert the reader to something questionable in the activity of the boat. By the end of the chapter, after the meeting with Rogue Riderhood, when Gaffer Hexam has composed himself 'into the easy attitude of one who had asserted the high moralities and taken an unassailable position'—he has with complete internal conviction made plain the difference between robbing the living and picking the pockets of the dead—we know not only what his trade is but that there is in him a moral coarseness which Lizzie for all her affection repudiates. The brief tight chapter realises a physical scene with great vividness and economy and at the same time conveys three distinct attitudes towards it. At only one point is there a sign of forcing, and that is just where the unwary seeker after Dickensian poetry may think he has most surely found it:

> it happened now, that a slant of light from the setting sun glanced into the bottom of the boat, and, touching a rotten stain there which bore some resemblance to the outline of a muffled human form, coloured it as though with diluted blood. This caught the girl's eye, and she shivered.

Here, we are plainly being told, is an image which will point to the heart of Lizzie's horror at what her father is doing. Of course it is quite possible that the boat could have had an innocent stain roughly of human shape and even that the sun's late rays should make it appear reddish. The picture itself is not false: what *is* is the way in which Dickens thrusts a dramatic interpretation on it— 'as though with diluted blood'—and presents this as of the girl's own vision: it seems like an attempt to force the reader to believe in her special sensitiveness by a piece of faked evidence, for the notion of blood comes obviously enough not from a fully understood young woman but from Dickens himself—he needs her to think like this and so he makes her do it. Yet the rest of the chapter comes directly out of intimate knowledge, intent only to realise it as exactly as possible.

Chapter i ends with Gaffer Hexam's display of self-satisfied uprightness. Chapter ii is full of the complacency of a very different social world, whose blindness comes in retrospect to seem oddly akin to that of the river-folk. The first paragraph is in a familiar vein:

> Mr. and Mrs. Veneering were bran-new people in a bran-new house in a bran-new quarter of London. Everything about the Veneerings was spick and span new. All their furniture was new, all their friends were new, all their servants were new, . . . they themselves were new, they were as newly married as was lawfully compatible with their having a bran-new baby, and if they had set up a great-grandfather, he would have come home in matting from the Pantechnicon, without a scratch upon him, French-polished to the crown of his head.

The effect is rhetorical comedy of a broad and simple kind, everything depending on the repetition of the one word 'new', and the building up of the long sentence to a climax which is neatly underplayed: for 'they themselves' are squeezed in at the end of a long list of their property (including their friends!), which is so much more obvious and notable than they are; and while they and everything else are bran-new, the reader naturally expects that, along with their baby, their marriage must be also. But propriety has even greater claims than newness: the baby is real and must be legally accounted for. As for the great-grandfather, though his image is ludicrous, this is not a pointless moment of farce—the extravagance of it clinches the brash smartness of the Veneerings: this is not only Society, but a shallow and trivial Society.

Though there has been an element of comedy in the encounter between Hexam and Riderhood, the irony with which Dickens invests the moment where Hexam establishes his sense of moral superiority (he had asserted the *high* moralities and taken an *unassailable* position—in his own eyes, that is) only distances the reader from the object to the extent of allowing him to stand back within the scene, to look at Hexam from a little way off but not from beyond the world in which he lives: this life has its pieties which may be smiled at but not mocked. In Chapter ii we have by contrast *satiric* comedy: the author here invites the reader to look at the Veneerings and their society from a point outside the frame of the thing seen; and the means used to achieve this distancing is exaggeration and the elimination of all the qualifying nuances which we know affect our direct vision of the real. Our experience of the superficiality of this world is concentrated in the word 'new': all the subsequent affected chatter at the dinner party emphasises this characteristic and no other. And whereas the honest reader may well ruefully recognise a tendency in himself akin to Hexam's complacency, he will never associate himself with the Veneerings. The approaches to the two so different scenes are therefore sharply opposed to one another. But there is more in the difference than a matter of method or even of the author's standpoint: the assumption behind it is of a difference in the essential nature of the two things seen—that Hexam's life, whether we like it or not, has a solidity, is in fact a way of living, which the other has not and is not; there may be corruption and fraud in the waterside life, but the Veneerings' society is *all* surface, and having no substance underneath is therefore a total fraud, a mere affected *imitation* of life, which the living reader cannot enter into and must look at from wholly outside.

So the opposition of the techniques in these two chapters is an expression of the extreme difference in the lives described. But Dickens goes one step further. Mortimer's story of the man from somewhere has introduced a potentially alien issue on to the shiny surface of the Veneering society; but to those present the new subject is merely a plaything which they toy with as with everything else: it enters in at this stage as something so remote that it can serve only as the occasion for titillation.

Now, however, at the start of Chapter iii Dickens brings the real into the unreal. The effect is striking and curiously disturbing; and the outcome is Mortimer's removal from the false glitter into the solid drabness of the real. He receives Charley Hexam, who brings with him a good deal of the coarseness of the river life as well as a rough education that cuts deeper than the superficial social culture, in a library full of 'bran-new books in bran-new bindings liberally gilded', at which Charley looks 'with an awakened curiosity that went below the binding'. The boy talks bluntly, without refinement, always on his guard; yet a certain vanity of his knowledge is revealed when he makes two allusions to the Bible to drive a point home—a vanity at an opposite pole to the affected ignorance of the dinner party. The dialogue between Mortimer and Charley, which has served also to bring out a straightforwardness in Mortimer distinguishing him from the rest of the company, is followed by his and Eugene's escape into a world in which they will find 'something really worth being energetic about'. And their talk, touched though it is by the affectation of boredom, shows a self-awareness and hence a possibility of escape from society triviality: they are not wholly beyond the influence of reality, and Eugene's story will tell of the painful and ultimately rewarding process by which he is led to accept it fully. So in a novel so much taken up with the confusion of appearance and reality, with the contrast between life and the imitation of life, the opening chapters establish these oppositions by a technique which impresses itself on the reader as being entirely at one with the object: the difference in the kinds of things seen determines the difference in the ways in which they *can* be seen.

(ii) SYMBOLISM

The river at the start of *Our Mutual Friend* is very much the real Thames, there in its own right. Yet already in the opening chapter there are indications that it stands for something beyond itself: Lizzie dislikes it because of her own special association with it. As her father gets his livelihood by finding bodies which the river has killed or helped to kill, it is a sign to her of an evil she shuns but cannot escape: yet it is also the provider—she is warmed by driftwood picked out of the river, the basket she slept in as a baby was washed ashore. So the river becomes a sign—a *symbol*—of conflicting elements in Lizzie's life, and the crises in her life all involve it. She insists she cannot turn her back on it when Charley (in his own interest) wishes to take her away from its influence. She still lives near it when later she is sent to the country. And at the great climax it becomes as nearly as possible both destroyer and provider in one action—in nearly encompassing the death of her lover, but giving the occasion on which her old skill, once used for ill, comes instinctively to her aid in saving life and purging the evil she has all along associated with the river. But of course the river is not itself evil. Bradley Headstone makes it his associate in an evil deed, just as in the past Lizzie's father's trade has darkened it for her: the character given to the river is then a symbol of the characteristic behaviour or nature of the people connected with it—evil in the case of Riderhood and Bradley Headstone, good in Lizzie's, ambiguous in her father's. Even so it remains, and this is important to its continuing to function as an effective symbol, the real living recognisable river. Occasionally perhaps Dickens attempts to make its symbolic character too obvious, and so it becomes simply a dead sign. How disastrous this can be is shown by contrast in a passage in *David Copperfield* which also uses the river but blatantly in an attempt to force the reader's moral sensibilities. 'Oh the river!' cries Martha, the fallen woman, over and over again:

> 'I know it's like me!' she exclaimed. 'I know that I belong to it. I know that it's the natural company of such as I am! It comes from country places, where there was once no harm in it—and it creeps through the dismal streets, defiled and miserable—and it goes away, like my life, to a great sea, that is always troubled—and I feel that I must go with it!' DC xlvii

And David comments that he has never known what despair was except in the tone of those words. What nonsense! The whole passage is a complete confection. The river is now merely an instrument to dramatise the girl's self-denigration; but the effect is utterly false, for it is incredible that Martha should in fact speak in such terms, or indeed feel what Dickens obliges her to. His attempt, by using the simile of the river, to solemnify her despair, only makes the reader feel he is being preached at. Nor does the image do anything to make the despair more graphic: there is in truth no river to be seen here, and the verbiage is inert and laboured, giving no life to the emotion that it is meant to evoke.

Quite a lot of Dickens's symbols remain inert, largely because he does not take the trouble to try to understand them for what they are in themselves. Thus the country is a standard resort for him—a place of purity and innocence in contrast to the corruption of the town. Sometimes there is evil in the country too; but in book after book, from *Oliver Twist* to *Our Mutual Friend*, the country is idealised as a place of recuperation or relief from the evil that the city engenders. Descriptions of the country are usually commonplace idealisations—cottages with roses round the door, cherubic children, comfortable and eccentric old doctors and retainers. It would not be fair to pretend that the sun is always shining in the country, but the air is customarily mild and friendly (see for instance Betty Higden's life in the pleasant riverside towns of Surrey, *OMF*, xli); and essentially the only evils are caused by the irruption of the town into the country—by Bradley Headstone stalking Eugene and Lizzie, by the London-bred poor laws or the spread of industry. Even in the marvellously subtle and perceptive *Great Expectations*, though the bleak landscape of the Kentish marshes is rendered without any false glow and though the country-town meannesses and trivialities are beautifully caught, life at the forge (despite Mrs. Gargery) has a rustic simplicity, which is of some importance to the moral patterning of the book (Orlick is a strange and alien intruder). Especially at the end this life has an innocence and jollity contrasted with the sophistication and false lights that turned Pip's head. Biddy and Joe live something like the ideal, innocent life, the loss of which is the cause of all Pip's troubles. Nowhere, even in this book, is there any hint of the squalor and poverty that hung over so much of rural England in the first half of the 19th century: Dickens had probably never seen it, and so he made a never-never-land of the English countryside, not interesting in itself because unreal, and in consequence ineffective as a symbol: it becomes so much dead weight to be carried by the experience it ought to illuminate.

It seems to me that several of Dickens's symbols suffer in this way. Apart from the river which really does live as an active participant in the book, *Our Mutual Friend* has another famous symbol—the dust from which the Harmon fortune comes. We must not think of dust in the fairly innocuous literal sense: here it refers to the heaps of dirt, ashes and decaying human dung which fouled large areas of London, but was so valuable as fertiliser that it could be sold at good profit. This as an emblem of the squalor out of which a fortune may grow—and grow to corrupt all who come into contact with it—is powerful and disgusting: its first appearance contrasts notably with the glitter of the riches of the Veneerings. The trouble is, however, that the dust-heaps which surround Boffin's Bower do not, despite Silas Wegg's poking about in them, play a truly active part in the story: they seem rather there to be heavily referred to when a larger meaning is required. So, when the heaps are being slowly cleared away, their symbolic significance is solemnly written in with an elaboration of the contemptuous phrase in *Hard Times* which characterises Parliament as the national dustmen:

> My lords and gentlemen and honourable boards, when you in the course of your dust-shovelling and cinder-raking have piled up a mountain of pretentious failure, you must off with your honourable coats for the removal of it, and fall to the work with the power of all the queen's horses and all the queen's men, or it will come rushing down and bury us alive.   OMF xli

But there is no dust of any sort, physical or moral, in *Our Mutual Friend* which carries that kind of threat: Boffin after all suffers no discomfort from living next to his heaps; and the heaps, which were a fine image to start with, have become an encumbrance which only serves to warn us when the author has palpable designs on us.

As Christopher Ricks has finely said (in his essay on *Great Expectations* in *Dickens and the Twentieth Century*), 'the important image or gesture or word should owe its existence to some non-symbolic necessity . . . to plausible characterisation, say, or likely incident.' It must indeed be more than just likely. A symbol that has been dragged into the narrative solely in order to emphasise or point out the larger significance of such-and-such an incident or character will give us inescapably the feeling that we are being nagged or prodded; and it is a sign of weakness in the narrative technique if such devices seem necessary. A small but characteristic example comes at the end of Chapter v of *Dombey and Son,* just after the excursion has been planned which will end in Paul's losing his foster-mother and ultimately all hope of a healthy childhood. Polly carried him to and fro to quiet him, feeling him to be cold:

> It was a bleak autumnal afternoon indeed; and as she walked, and hushed, and, glancing through the dreary windows, pressed the little fellow closer to her breast, the withered leaves came showering down.

There is nothing unlikely in the coincidence of Susan Nipper's daring scheme and a blustery autumn day; but the reader knows immediately that the stale image of the falling leaves is only there to make Paul's plight appear all the sadder and his prospects the more hopeless: sure enough the next chapter brings it all out.

Forced symbolism of this kind can be found in most of Dickens's novels, and it can be severely damaging. Famous as it is, the whole symbolic apparatus of *Bleak House* seems to me to be attached to the narrative by factitious contrivance: there is altogether too much art and not enough nature about it. Consider Esther's reflexion as she watches Richard Carstone driving off from Lincolnshire with the sombre Vholes:

> I shall never forget those two seated side by side in the lantern's light—Richard, all flush and fire and laughter, with the reins in his hand; Mr. Vholes, quite still, black gloved, and buttoned up, looking at him as if he were looking at his prey and charming it. I have before me the whole picture of the warm dark night, the summer lightning, the dusty track of road closed in by hedgerows and high trees, the gaunt pale horse with his ears pricked up, and the driving away at speed to Jarndyce and Jarndyce. BH xxxvii

This is particularly regrettable. For not only does Dickens force the symbolic significance of Vholes (who immediately before has been given a sympathetic aspect through his care for his father and daughters, and who is elsewhere impressively realised for the bleak and characteristic exponent of dead law that that law would naturally surround itself with), and add the gaunt pale horse for good (or bad) measure; but he falsifies his narrative by being obliged to give to Esther an insight and attitude towards experience which are foreign to her nature and habit, and are plainly Dickens's own: his desire to inject meaning into the incident has led him to corrupt the presentation of his narrator-heroine on whom so much depends.

If this instance were unique or nearly so, it would not matter much. But in the fact the whole endless paraphernalia of Chancery, which is itself a symbol for the great modern curse of the dead weight of meaningless formality, protocol, officialdom and rules, is surrounded by a great company of symbolic contraptions, each of which by itself may have momentary piquancy and force, but which in sum make a framework of nearly fatal rigidity. There is Krook's second-hand shop which, with its ever unsorted mountains of rubbish which is never cleared out, is explicitly likened to the Court of Chancery and whose owner is nicknamed the Lord Chancellor, partly for his unwillingness to part with anything which has once come into his hands (Chapter v). There is Miss Flyte, always expecting judgment, on the Day of Judgment, as a perpetual reminder, to Richard and the rest, of what getting trapped by the law will bring one to—with her symbolically named birds, Hope, Joy, Youth, etc., all caged together and not to be released until she receives judgment. And of course there is the fog. Everyone who has heard of Dickens and symbolism together knows about the fog in *Bleak House*. But the part it plays in the novel has been greatly exaggerated. It only appears twice, but the first time is at the very start of the book and readers have been duly overwhelmed:

> Smoke lowering down from the chimney-pots, making a soft black drizzle, with flakes of soot in it as big as full-grown snowflakes— gone into mourning, one might imagine, for the death of the sun.

That is a happy pleasantry and, being gone in a moment, does not overstay its welcome. Then the fog settles in, the word repeated over and again to enforce a sense of its omnipresence, and then the inescapable moral rubbed in:

> The raw afternoon is rawest, and the dense fog is densest, and the muddy streets are muddiest, near that leaden-headed old obstruction, appropriate ornament for the threshold of a leaden-headed old corporation—Temple Bar. And hard by Temple Bar, in Lincoln's Inn Hall, at the very heart of the fog, sits the Lord Chancellor in his High Court of Chancery.
>
> Never can there come fog too thick, never can there come mud and mire too deep, to assort with the groping and floundering condition which this High Court of Chancery, most pestilent of hoary sinners, holds, this day, in the sight of heaven and earth.

Dickens is of course deeply concerned in *Bleak House* with the grimness and physical corruption of London. Yet the real fog is no essential part of the story, any more than the rain at Chesney Wold, which sorts so well with Lady Dedlock's boredom. It is there, not because London is necessarily the place of bad weather, but because it is the place of corruption and must have weather to match. One's complaint is not that the fog is an inapt image for the fog of Chancery and in particular the inextricable muddle of Jarndyce and Jarndyce, but that it remains a mere inert statement of an image, unable, after the first announcement of itself, to add life to its subject.

By contrast there are images, symbolic of the theme of a novel, which become a framework for the whole narrative structure of the book, their moral significance growing as the story grows, the junction between the two remaining always easy and natural. At the end of the first chapter of *Great Expectations,* Pip watches the convict walking away,

> hugging his shuddering body in both his arms—clasping himself, as if to hold himself together . . . picking his way among the nettles, and among the brambles that bound the green mounds [of the churchyard], he looked in my young eyes as if he were eluding the hands of the dead people, stretching up cautiously out of their graves, to get a twist upon his ankle and pull him in.

Then Pip sees him go on further, towards the gibbet with chains that had once held a pirate.

> The man was limping on towards this latter, as if he were the pirate come to life, and come down, and going back to hook himself up again.

There is nothing obviously symbolic here—just a frightened child's imagination playing on a scene unforgettably vivid in all its detail. Yet the movement of the convict as he seems carefully to elude the pull of the grave to go and hang himself symbolises in miniature the whole unifying theme which relates the various stories within the novel.

A more obviously notable instance is the sequence of prisons in *Little Dorrit* (see pp. 148–51)—a composite and highly complex metaphor comprising not only the physical presence of the Marshalsea which dominates so much of the book, but the self-inflicted prison of Mrs. Clennam's room, the sense of London itself, especially Bleeding Heart Yard, the inextricable tangle of red tape in the Circumlocution Office, right down to grim little details like the Merdles' gaoler-like butler and Mr. Merdle hugging himself as if taking himself into custody. The central theme of the book is obsession, the imprisonment of men within ideas of their own making—a theme explored and dramatised most fully in Mr. Dorrit and Mrs. Clennam, but enclosing so many of the others, from Miss Wade with her sour sense of permanent grievance against the world deriving from her notion that she cannot be loved, to Pancks, caught up in his unimpeachable figures which nevertheless cause such disaster. And all along the physical restrictions, within which so much of the necessarily largely abortive action takes place, are a physical emblem of the trap that people in the book have sprung on themselves.

Hard Times is a symbolically conceived novel of a different kind. Gradgrind is presented at the start as an almost caricatured representative of an attitude to life which can be, somewhat inadequately, summed up in the word 'materialism', expressed as a desire to reduce the whole world to a concentration on 'Facts'. The theme of the novel is the crippling effect on life of carrying this philosophy into action, and its final, appallingly costly, defeat by what has previously been derogatorily dismissed as fancy or sentiment. In *Hard Times* both the physical environment—the hideously depressing Coketown—and the moral nature of the protagonists are laid down by the application of the philosophy of facts. Yet so inevitably does the action grow from the premisses of this philosophy, that one is hardly conscious as one reads that certain characters and situations act on us symbolically as well as realistically. This is, I think, because the principal characters are not conceived as symbols and then given certain actions to perform; they are seen as particular human beings, but such is the nature of Dickens's peculiar kind of perceptiveness that he instinctively sees and conveys them to us as *representative*. He sees in each not only the individuality which every person must have or cease to be a person, but that they are in certain respects essentially typical as well (for no two human beings can be so alike as to be indistinguishable, and no two can be so different as to share no common characteristics). Bitzer is presented patently as the perfection of a type; but even Sissy, who is equally plainly offered as Bitzer's exact opposite, with her spontaneous, uncalculating generosity and good will, has her archetypal quality: it is she who at two great crises can save the Gradgrind family from total collapse and disintegration, and she can do this because it is of the nature of unselfish goodness to be outgoing and restorative. When at the final dénouement she manages to smuggle Tom away to Sleary, we feel that it is natural she should know from her bent and upbringing where the circus is, and further that there is an instinctive companionship between those 'incapable of any kind of sharp practice' which can be relied on at the particular juncture where it is needed and called out. And it is of the nature of the typical that it should be predictable and so in this extended sense reliable.

(iii) SYMBOLS AND TYPES

In order to understand the working of Dickens's symbolic imagination, it is important to realise that, in characterisation at any rate, symbol and type are closely connected. The characters which in one's earliest acquaintance with Dickens one is apt to take hold of most firmly are those that appear at first merely odd or idiosyncratic—Mrs. Gamp, Pickwick, Jenny Wren, Captain Cuttle: such figures seem to have established themselves as eminently 'Dickensian'. But they do not represent the real strength of his art; rather are they by-products of the super-abundant energy which is one of the sure indications of the great human inclusiveness we so much value, but which is always threatening to run away with the main line of the book. Yet we find him by contrast accused of being able to invent nothing but grotesque parodies, or at best diagrams, of humanity. At times plainly he means to produce diagrams—to show what happens to humanity when all its humanising characteristics are eliminated. Almost always such vignettes (they are not normally more) are immediately recognisable by their names, which are themselves deliberate parodies—Mr. McChoakumchild, Mr. Tite Barnacle. But many of Dickens's names have symbolic intent, being suggestive and associative rather than directly revelatory, characterising more or less obliquely the particular weakness, affectation or vanity which is their owner's peculiar claim on our attention. Gradgrind and Bounderby alert us to crucial aspects of their natures; Bitzer sounds like a terrier; Veneering brilliantly contains the whole man within a word—he has nothing but veneer, but the smoothness and balance of the name suggest too an easy, slippery movement within society. Turvey-drop works on us more indirectly, reinforcing rather than initiating the impression of pompous self-importance which we gain from his speech and actions.

Physical appearance is also frequently used symbolically by Dickens. Miss Murdstone, who becomes almost literally a gaoler to David Copperfield, had

> very heavy eyebrows, nearly meeting over her large nose, as if, being disabled by the wrongs of her sex from wearing whiskers, she had carried them to that account. She brought with her two uncompromising hard black boxes, with her initials on the lids in hard brass nails. When she paid the coachman she took her money out of a hard steel purse, and she kept the purse in a very jail of a

bag which hung upon her arm by a heavy chain, and shut up like a bite. I had never, at that time, seen such a metallic lady altogether as Miss Murdstone was. DC iv

The most consummate instance of all is the contrast between Sissy and Bitzer in Chapter ii of *Hard Times*—Sissy dark and lustrous and pulsating with spontaneous life, Bitzer so pale that all life seems to have been washed out of him (see further pp. 134–5). Of course Dickens is not saying that human characteristics necessarily or characteristically show themselves in physical appearance: the function of these descriptions is symbolic—to intensify or vivify the reader's appreciation of the human qualities the character is there to represent. There is at least one instance, however, where it seems to me that Dickens deliberately uses a physical impression to work up an emotional state of disgust in the reader, as if he feels so vicious towards his character that he must write in something that will make us dislike him morally even more than we do already. This occurs when Uriah Heep obliges David Copperfield to put him up in his flat, and David is so obsessed with him that he keeps returning to look at him. Heep is of course an exceptionally unpleasant character anyway, but when David (in the first person of course —we are supposed to take it as 'the truth') describes him as 'lying on his back, with his legs extending to I don't know where, gurglings taking place in his throat, stoppages in his nose, and his mouth open like a post-office' (*DC,* xxv), the effect is of Dickens (via David) twisting the reader's arm; and the reader's reaction may on the contrary be to wonder what is wrong with David that he 'could not help wandering in and out every half-hour or so, and taking another look at him'. It is far from Dickens's conscious intention that David's preoccupation with Uriah's physical repulsiveness should seem obsessive: what in fact must lie behind this unattractive episode is a desire to make us shudder all the more when Uriah comes to aspire to Agnes's hand, and so by compensation feel David all the more fitting as her final match.

Since such names and appearances are associated with the

characters of the persons who bear them, it will be a natural consequence if the characters remain static. This is not always the case with such symbolically named and conceived figures—Gradgrind is an obvious instance to the contrary, for by the end of the book he is a changed man—but, as with the figures of virtues and vices in the old morality plays, it is generally the function of a symbolic figure in Dickens to remain an unchanging and recognisable mark. So Turveydrop is seen in new situations, which give new opportunities for the display of his self-centred vanity, but there is no notion of growth or development associated with him. So it is with Mrs. Skewton, Mrs. General, Mr. Boythorn, Sloppy. I want to insist that it is not—or not necessarily—a limitation, a sign of wilting imagination, that such figures remain so consistently predictable and limited. For they represent a diagrammatic picture of the total world, a chart of stylised human possibilities, among which the main characters move. *Bleak House* is made up very largely of such figures; their function is wholly representative, even though they may be and often are given idiosyncratic tricks by which they are instantly recognised. It is really no more than an apparent paradox that these figures, which are so insistently typical in conception and function, are marked out by oddities which belong to them alone: for the oddity, if it is successful, is simply a particular expression of the characteristic which it is their job to embody, a characteristic often marked out with delicacy and precision. Consider Mrs. General and Mrs. Sparsit. They are obviously closely related: snobbery is probably the first word one would think of to describe them; both toady to those more powerful than themselves, indeed they live off them; and the function of both in the developing theme of each novel is to display and exercise their snobbery. But it is not enough to call them both snobs and leave it at that: Mrs. Sparsit has a fairly robust vulgarity in her attachment to title, which she uses to keep her end up with Bounderby—hers is a class snobbery; Mrs. General's is rather a snobbery of money, and her bullying takes the form of a mincing gentility. So their different outward habits are the visible signs of different moral functions within the artistic whole of the novel. And perhaps the same is true even of Snagsby: he has a weak benevolence which is often overcome by the timid subservience he feels toward those in positions of superior power; and his prim turns of speech underline the weakness and timidity together.

It is often easy enough to summarise the characteristics which go to make up a Dickensian character. So many of them fall into recognisable categories; and fairly simple generalisations seem adequate. Yet for many of those figures that seem at first to drop into familiar and simple types, such categorisation will represent a serious distortion. Dickens's thought does obviously fall into patterns almost as a matter of course: he sees people essentially from the outside and in broad straightforward outline; it is his great mark to be exceptionally alive to people's behaviour, but not necessarily to understand it. Yet the patterns are by no means always predictable. The reader moving quickly from one novel to another will often find familiar faces; for Dickens's characters have a habit of falling into family groups or clusters; and the unwary may assume too quickly that one member of a family is just like another. There is for example a cluster of superior young men with the superficial character of a gentleman, a great affectation of boredom and a parade of outward honesty with no emotional sincerity beneath: James Harthouse and Henry Gowan are obviously very like one another (Gowan is outwardly the more unscrupulous), and both perhaps owe something to Steerforth and give something to Bentley Drummle and even to Eugene Wrayburn. The last-mentioned, however, who is gradually proved to have a heart that can be touched to real feeling, shows what a variety Dickens manages within a single general type; and this might then make one ponder whether the easy brilliance, the bland but self-centred and emotionally cowardly nature of Steerforth is not something else again. There are many other clusters worth considering for the sameness and difference of their members, for instance the selfishly ambitious who have a very strong sense of their own rights and others' duties: Edward Dorrit and Tom Gradgrind, Martin Chuzzlewit and Charley Hexam. And again, one of the most interesting clusters of all, the rough, unpolished professional man usually with a very un-prepossessing exterior, who yet has a sense of honour and straight dealing which proves more reliable in the end than so many overt professions of good will that remain merely professions. Newman Noggs is a prototype here, and the group brings together Inspector Bucket, Pancks, Wemmick and, perhaps most intriguingly, Sleary. In each case the reader's first impression is likely to be distinctly unfavourable, and the grounds for this dislike and distrust are never done away with—Pancks remains dirty, Sleary is always brandy-soaked—but they are seen to be insignificant against the larger humanity which makes these men truly honourable. So they are living protests against judging over-rapidly from exterior impressions. This in itself makes one realise how short-sighted it is to think of Dickens's perception as being narrowly categorical and the outcome in his novels a mere matter of rearranging unchanging types into new patterns. For over and again one may think one knows all round a Dickens character and have him neatly docketed in an analytical pigeon-hole, only to find that one's judgment has been premature. Even so patent a figure of fun as Major Bagstock has, we suddenly find, a low shrewdness which enables him to see round, if not through, Mr. Dombey.

A more important and notable case is that of Sir Leicester Dedlock. He is Dickens's solidest and most substantial representative of an entrenched traditional conservatism which seems always on the edge of toppling over into absurdity. Faced with the down-to-earth ironmaster Mr. Rouncewell, the son of his own housekeeper, whom he sees as a threat to all he stands for, Sir Leicester becomes 'very magnificent'. When Mr. Rouncewell observes, with conventional politeness, that he need not comment on the value to him of Lady Dedlock's kind opinion of the girl his son wants to marry, ' "That", observes Sir Leicester with unspeakable grandeur, for he thinks the ironmaster a little too glib, "must be quite unnecessary." ' (*BH,* xxviii.) And when the ironmaster's intentions of 'educating other people out of their stations' become inescapably plain to him, he sees the future in terms of 'obliterating the landmarks, and opening the floodgates'—grotesque metaphors to which he habitually resorts because he is too blinded by his sense of station and tradition to see reality as it is. Yet he has a 'habitual regard for truth', and when it is brought before him acknowledges its superior claims on him. And absurd though its expression normally is, he is completely honourable: this finally makes even his pompous formality impressive when he is faced with the great crisis of the disclosure of Lady Dedlock's past and her flight:

> 'My Lady is too high in position, too handsome, too accomplished, too superior in most respects to the best of those by whom she is surrounded, not to have her enemies and traducers, I dare say. Let it be known to them, as I make it known to you, that being of sound mind, memory, and understanding, I revoke no disposition I have made in her favour. I abridge nothing I have ever bestowed upon her. I am on unaltered terms with her; and I recall—having the full power to do it if I were so disposed, as you see—no act I have done for her advantage and happiness.'

> His formal array of words might have at any other time, as it has often had, something ludicrous in it; but at this time it is serious and affecting. His noble earnestness, his fidelity, his gallant shielding of her, his generous conquest of his own wrong and his own pride for her sake, are simply honourable, manly, and true.   BH lviii

Finally in the case of Sleary in *Hard Times* we have, very daringly, the deliberate use of a superficially unattractive figure to bear the weight of most of the moral principle of the story's theme—'a stout man . . . with one fixed eye and one loose eye, a voice (if it can be called so) like the efforts of a broken old pair of bellows, a flabby surface, and a muddled head which was never sober and never drunk' (*HT*, vi). His name, which suggests a mixture of 'bleary' and 'sleazy', seems designed to remind us constantly of his flabby exterior and his always being in drink. At the point in the penultimate chapter when he delivers the formal statement of the book's moral, he reminds us himself that he always takes brandy-and-water and seems to draw his inspiration from the depths of his glass. Yet, deplorable as his outward appearance is, we know from the start that he is motivated by a disinterested and spontaneous generosity which does not simply redeem the half-drunk flabbiness, but renders it irrelevant, of no account. What matters, as Mrs. Skewton might have said, is heart; and Sleary's heart is completely sound: only the snob will condemn him for his outside.

Indeed it may be said that this whole tendency in Dickens which I have just been looking at—the tendency to resist easy categorisation—is anti-snobbish. Snobbery may be defined as the basing of judgments of value on arbitrary distinctions: the social snob puts high value on birth and class and regards inferiority in these as the criterion of a lower human worth; similarly with the intellectual or money snob—which is not of course to say that intellectual qualities are not themselves of great human value. This concern with snobbery becomes more intense towards the end of Dickens's life. His last two complete novels are largely concerned with it in that they explore the fundamental question of what kind of things make human life valuable. *Great Expectations* is the story of Pip's painful and costly voyage of discovery from the crudity of worshipping Estella because she has money and social poise and despising Joe because he has not, to the point of recognising in loyalty, fidelity, constancy and selfless love things of infinitely more value than those for which he ignored or neglected them in the past. The plot of *Our Mutual Friend* is much more involved and the novel in consequence less single-mindedly concentrated on one central theme; yet it is plain that in both main stories Dickens is concerned to champion these same qualities of selflessness and faithfulness against the social attitudes which are summed up in the Veneerings' last party, when Twemlow so memorably vindicates Eugene's marriage to Lizzie: it is a question, he insists, of the feelings of a gentleman, who is made the greater gentleman by acting out of gratitude, respect, admiration and affection (*OMF,* lxvii). It is a new statement of what is certainly the strongest positive motivation in Dickens's art, and may be compared with the equally admirable moment near the end of *Dombey and Son* when Cousin Feenix overcomes his native debility to conjure Edith not to stop half way, but to set right, as far as she can, whatever she has done wrong—not for the honour of her family, not for her own fame, not for any of those considerations which unfortunate circumstances have induced her to regard as hollow, and in point of fact as approaching to humbug—but because it *is* wrong, and not right.   D & S lxi

At this moment, Dickens tells us with just the right touch of additional emphasis and specificity, 'a real and genuine earnestness [shone] through the levity of his manner and his slipshod speech'.

(iv) SATIRE

Dickens, then, gives us many examples both of the type figure and of the anti-type that upsets familiar categories and distinctions. The first kind may be presented directly or symbolically and is characteristically associated with satire, a mode which Dickens employs fitfully in many books and which gives us in *Martin Chuzzlewit* his one example (apart from the unclassifiable *Pickwick*) of an overall comic novel. Dickens's comedy, where it is not mere exuberance and fun, is characteristically satirical. I shall not here attempt a strict definition of satire, which, as Mr. Squeers said of nature, is more easily conceived than described, but shall limit myself to saying to start with that it always tends to involve a sense of the ridiculous or contradictory: it takes a steady, concentrated gaze at folly or vice by which they are made above all to appear absurd and to involve those who practise them in behaviour which is self-contradictory in that, of its nature, it defeats its own ends. In Swift's *Modest Proposal for Preventing the Children of Ireland from being a Burden to their Parents or Country*, the proposal turns out to be far from modest—an outrage on human sentiment; but Swift's point is that his proposal is in fact less outrageous than the seemingly far more innocent way in which Ireland is treated as it is, and that those who are shocked by the one but practise the other are not only insensitive and cruel but also irrational. Moreover they are (perhaps unconscious) hypocrites. Hypocrisy is an obvious target for satire, for it involves contradiction by its definition—a want of continuity between profession and practice.

61

Dickens's satire is rarely as complex or mercurial as Swift's; his exposure of hypocrisy is often nearer to invective than satire. There is little enough to laugh at in the clash between the benign patriarchal appearance of Mr. Casby and the vicious way in which he makes Pancks screw his poor tenants. Yet if one compares the final exposure of Casby (*LD* II, xxxii) with that of, say, Ralph Nickleby (*NN,* lx), one sees immediately that Casby's end is the subject of comedy—his appearance becomes ludicrous and his pretensions a patent fake. It is in any case a mistake to regard comedy as necessarily a laughing matter (there is nothing funny about the *Modest Proposal*); and Dickens's satire has a great range of tone, from the cheerfully mocking (Chadband) through the uneasy and ambiguous (not allowing the reader to settle easily down—Pumblechook) to the bitter and mordant (Mrs. Skewton).

When Dickens reduces politics to dust and calls Parliament the national cinder-heap, he is working within the same range of techniques as Swift, when in *Gulliver's Travels* he parodies political differences as quarrels about which end one should open a boiled egg. But the satirical *novelist* typically creates *figures* of satire; and his typical method is caricature. Caricature, by exaggerating attitudes and the habitual expression of them, makes all the plainer the contradictoriness that I have been stressing: Mrs. Pardiggle's philanthropic work and intentions are shown to be not only false but ridiculous in the light of the 'voluntary contributions' she exacts from her resentful children (*BH,* viii). When one looks closely at how he speaks and at his antics with his eye-glass, Young Barnacle seems obviously a parody of an official blinded by red tape (*LD* I, x, xvii). But even here the exaggeration is rather in manner than in substance. And Dickens's finest satirical portraits are arguably not caricatures at all. Bounderby is perhaps the most complete of these. Ruskin, who admired *Hard Times* very greatly, nevertheless thought Bounderby overdrawn; but again the elements of parody appear rather in expression than in sentiment or attitude—the repeated phrase about turtle soup and venison, not the bullying or the overweening sense of his own rights and importance. He is a hypocrite of a special and comprehensive kind, his whole life being based on a fraud (see p. 143), and his exposure is an occasion of sardonic comedy, the relish of which Mrs. Sparsit brings out when she interrupts his mock-modest reference to his 'poor judgment'—

> 'Oh! Pray, sir, . . . don't disparage your judgment. Everybody knows how unerring Mr. Bounderby's judgment is. Everybody has had proofs of it. It must be the theme of general conversation. Disparage anything in yourself but your judgment, sir.' HT xxxvii

(This closing chapter of *Hard Times* is a masterpiece of ironic exposure: note especially the dialogue in which Bounderby and Mrs. Sparsit score off one another, each in a vain attempt to recover some dignity and self-esteem. This is Mrs. Sparsit's closing speech:

> 'If that portrait could speak, sir—but it has the advantage over the original of not possessing the power of committing itself and disgusting others—it would testify, that a long period has elapsed since I first habitually addressed it as the picture of a noodle. Nothing that a noodle does can awaken surprise or indignation; the proceedings of a noodle can only inspire contempt.' HT xxxvii

It undoubtedly tells on Bounderby, but equally against her. Though she sweeps past him 'with her Roman features struck like a medal to commemorate her scorn of Mr. Bounderby', she has to eat some very sour grapes—her speech is a vain attempt to regain by scornful words a position of superiority from which she has been toppled.)

The novelist's satire, however, though it must work through particular figures, whether caricatured or not, is not directed at these figures: the object of satire is the exposure, through ridicule, of contemptible or deplorable attitudes or behaviour. Obviously these must in a novel be expressed in character—they must be the attitudes and behaviour of someone active in the story. And for this reason of course satire deals in the type-figure, depending necessarily on static characterisation. The object satirised need not be closely attached to a particular character, though—if only that it may be quickly identified for what it is—normally it will be, particularly in a novelist with Dickens's naturally schematic habits of mind. Such 'characters' necessarily get stuck within the definition that they start with, for their function in the novel is simply to display certain characteristics and show them at work.

This fixity of characterisation has been made the grounds of a charge against Dickens which essentially amounts to one of determinism: his characters, it is said, are born basically either good or bad, and have no chance, if not born good, of ever becoming so. Worse still, Dickens, having created 'bad' people who cannot escape their badness, sneers at them for being hypocrites or cheats. This seems to me to represent a serious misunderstanding of the nature of the art with which we are here concerned. As a matter of fact Dickens does give us people redeemed from folly or evil or weakness—Pip, Mr. Gradgrind, Mr. Dombey, Eugene Wrayburn. To achieve something like a realistic portrayal of such a change, the characters must to some extent at least be seen from the inside (it is partly because Dickens seems to have a merely notional idea of what Martin Chuzzlewit is like as a person that his conversion is so nominal and uninteresting); and they must be given something like the complexity of human reality. Satire on the other hand involves deliberate distortion by simplification, to concentrate on a single object, and so cannot afford to dull its effect by giving a realistic extrapolation from experience: it is a highly specialised selection to very special ends. Its object is not people but patterns of behaviour, habits of mind; and the characters of satire are created simply to house these, and not at all for their own sakes. Consider Mr. Podsnap, perhaps the most splendid of all Dickens's satirical inventions. He has given us a new word—Podsnappery—to indicate the particular brand of complacent chauvinistic snobbery which is the one thing that everyone remembers about him because it is the one characteristic he has. Of course no one will believe that a real person could exist with only this: that is not the point—Podsnap exists only for the sake of Podsnappery, and it is this that is Dickens's target in the wonderful passage in Chapter xi of *Our Mutual Friend* in which it is displayed in its fullest splendour (a passage whose impact is immediate and stands in no need of detailed exposition, but which incidentally is one of those that reveal how immensely so much of Dickens gains from being read aloud). No character in literature exists except in terms of what is told or implied in the book in which he comes; it is a characteristic of satire to tell all and imply nothing; and a pre-occupation with satirical figures as if they were solid people of whom only a sketch has been given and much left out betrays a false conception of the relation of this kind of art to the life with which it is ultimately and deeply concerned. Here—in Podsnap—Dickens says, is chauvinism, uncomplicated by any of the multitude of details which could accompany it in the real: to be worried over Podsnap's inability to escape from Podsnappery is to be worried over folly's inability to become wisdom; it is to confuse the sin with the sinner and the fool with his folly.

Podsnap, in short, is not a person at all: he is a dramatised attitude, a vice or humour. It is of the nature of satire at its purest to be above a concern with persons; when we meet with a feeling which seems aimed more at a given person we are likely to be moving away from satire to something else. Dickens creates a good many characters towards whom he openly displays the strongest feelings, as of contempt (Miss Monflathers) or bitter scorn (Grandfather Smallweed). On reading the piece of savagery about Mrs. Skewton quoted above (p. 36), one may well react above all, 'How he hates her!'—the sarcasm seems to have become vindictive and to be directed not at the exposure of hypocrisy but at the humiliation of the hypocrite: it has lost the aspect of impersonality essential to true satire.

This impersonality makes itself clear in Dickens's readiness to use characters who are themselves the objects of his irony as protagonists of his attacks on cant and bogusness. Harthouse, the fashionable cynic, replies to Mrs. Sparsit's trite conventionality, 'We live in a singular world', with a mock compliment which to the reader, though not to Mrs. Sparsit, shatters all her pretensions to good sense:

> 'I have had the honour, by a coincidence of which I am proud, to have made a remark, similar in effect, though not so epigrammatically expressed.'   HT XXV

No one is to suppose from this that Dickens is relenting towards Harthouse, whose heart he later calls a 'nest of addled eggs'; but his rottenness does not prevent his making the appropriate comment on Mrs. Sparsit's thick-headed gentility, for he has intelligence, though he misuses it.

Martin Chuzzlewit is the nearest Dickens gets to writing a satirical novel, though of course it contains very different elements as well—the sentimental haze which surrounds the Pinches, the violent melodrama of Jonas Chuzzlewit and Tigg Montague, the perfunctory story of Martin's moral education through illness (Dickens is not interested in Martin himself). And it can be argued that in the one section of the novel to which Dickens is wholly committed and deeply involved, he does not altogether trust the power of his satire and must formalise the statement of his own attitudes in various positive and more or less explicit ways. Everyone can see that the whole American section of the novel comes out of his strong reaction to his own trip to the United States in 1842. At times the picture of the American scene becomes lampoon, as in the wild extravagance of this great gobble of food:

> The oysters, stewed and pickled, leaped from their capacious reservoirs, and slid by scores into the mouths of the assembly. The sharpest pickles vanished, whole cucumbers at once, like sugar-plums, and no man winked his eye. Great heaps of indigestible matter melted away as ice before the sun. It was a solemn and an awful thing to see. Dyspeptic individuals bolted their food in wedges; feeding, not themselves, but broods of nightmares, who were continually standing at livery within them. . . .   MC xvi

This obviously stands on its own feet and has no need of comment from Dickens or his hero, who is present simply as an observer. On more serious issues, however, Dickens seems to feel his touch less secure. In Chapter xvii Martin is introduced to the 'liberal-minded' Norris family, who nevertheless find Negroes ridiculous. Enter the renowned democrat, General Fladdock, fresh from a trip to England and full of 'the exclusiveness, the pride, the form, the ceremony . . . the artificial barriers set up between man and man; the division of the human race into court cards and plain cards of every denomination—into clubs, diamonds, spades—anything but hearts!' But of course there is appalled consternation when it turns out that Martin came over in the steerage: the democratic pretensions are instantly laid bare as a fraud. And then, as if to excuse himself from the charge of partiality Dickens brings back his 'good American', Bevan, not only as a reminder of the standards by which the Norrises are found wanting, but also explicitly to reinforce the intention of the episode with the expression of a very 'European' point of view. Again, when Martin attends a meeting of the Watertoast Association of United Sympathisers, the meeting ends in uproar when it is discovered that the Irishman with whom the association is sympathising for his opposition to the British Lion turns out to be a consistent advocate of 'nigger emancipation'. The point is broad and clear: it is made sharper by Dickens's shrewd observation of the effect of the repeated use of the symbolic animals, lion and eagle, which turn the opposition into a mere charade: no real encounter is ever contemplated. But at the end of the episode Martin himself must deliver a formal moral when he sees the republican flag which had been hoisted in honour of the farce at which he has been present. 'Tut! You're a gay flag in the distance. But let a man be near enough to get the light upon the other side, and see through you, and you are but sorry fustian!' (*MC*, xxi) (a neat play on the two meanings of the word). Curiously enough, however, despite these somewhat partial aids that he has called in, so strong is Dickens's feeling about what America seems to him to involve, and so insistently does he sense the threat that he feels it to represent, that at one point (Chapter xxii) he patently steps out of the novel and in a piece of very forceful polemical prose which foreshadows the political writing of Matthew Arnold, makes a formal statement of his own position. It is a moment of considerable solemnity and in its way impressiveness; yet it reveals inescapably that in these sections at least Dickens is essentially using the novel as a vehicle—not letting his mind play freely over experience, not letting experience present itself, but overtly insisting on the way in which we are to receive it.

How different is the treatment of Pecksniff, whose doings really have a larger share in the story than Martin's. Here Dickens is on more familiar ground, feeling no need to establish formally where he stands: he could take for granted his English readers' acquaintance with Pecksniffs all around them. Pecksniff is Dickens's lengthiest satirical portrait, the nature and interest of which are made clear on his first appearance:

> Mr. Pecksniff was a moral man. . . . Perhaps there never was a more moral man than Mr. Pecksniff, especially in his conversation and correspondence. It was once said of him by a homely admirer, that he had a Fortunatus's purse of good sentiments in his inside. In this particular he was like the girl in the fairy tale, except that if they were not actual diamonds which fell from his lips, they were the very brightest paste, and shone prodigiously. He was a most exemplary man; fuller of virtuous precept than a copy-book. Some people likened him to a direction-post, which is always telling the way to a place, and never goes there: but these were his enemies; the shadows cast by his brightness—that was all. MC ii

(Fortunatus was the legendary hero whose purse, a gift from the goddess of Fortune, was replenished as often as he drew from it.) Pecksniff plainly enough is a hypocrite through and through. Though I have resisted the argument that it is necessarily a weakness that such a character should be seen by his author as unalterably a hypocrite, there is more force in the charge that essentially the truth about Pecksniff is revealed in the first two or three chapters, and that the rest merely play variations on what we already know. Yet this too seems to me somewhat unjust, even though it may be granted that Dickens was unwise to draw Pecksniff out to such length: where the object of satire is unchanging, the very long look becomes superfluous, and Pecksniff is too much concerned with playing a part and not enough with developing an idea. Still, while Pecksniff remains a bland and pretentious hypocrite through the book, the nature and consequences of his hypocrisy *are* progressively revealed. In the splendid scene of the family gathering in Chapter iv, we find for instance that though, as we are beginning to realise, Pecksniff is above all greedy and covetous (he 'will not remember' the existence of money), his way is to present himself as excessively for-bearing, while doing his best to score off his adversaries at the same time:

> 'Pecksniff', said Anthony [Chuzzlewit], who had been watching the whole party with peculiar keenness from the first, 'don't you be a hypocrite.'
> 'A what, my good sir?' demanded Mr. Pecksniff.
> 'A hypocrite.'
> 'Charity, my dear', said Mr. Pecksniff, 'when I take my chamber candlestick tonight, remind me to be more than usually particular in praying for Mr. Anthony Chuzzlewit, who has done me an injustice.'
> This was said in a very bland voice, and aside, as being addressed to his daughter's private ear.

Only gradually does the viciousness which is Pecksniff's real nature show itself: he does not simply want to appear better than he is: he uses his cloak of meekness as a cover for the ugliness of his schemes and intentions. These are slowly revealed until the point (Chapter xxx) where he openly blackmails Mary by threatening to ruin Martin: this is when (as he thinks) he has attained a position of complete power and can shed pretence, and this is what the pretence is not only designed to conceal: it is also a bait to trap the innocent and supposedly unwary. Yet even here, when Pecksniff reveals himself, he maintains in his speech a skin of apparent thoughtfulness and courtesy which makes his bullying all the more repellent. This does not constitute any change or development in Pecksniff's character: what we have is rather a progressive revelation of it and, in particular through the lamentable careers of his daughters, of its influence for evil on those over whom it gains real power. The story is the story of his over-reaching himself; and perhaps the theme becomes somewhat too blatant, when Dickens feels he must humiliate Pecksniff at the end, much as he has humiliated Bumble before.

(v) CHARACTERISATION

In any novel character is only—to use a philosophical term—a logical construction out of the language which the author selects to describe or evoke it. Whereas the description of a real person may in principle be checked against the person himself, in a novel there is nothing beyond what the author chooses to give and imply. Our awareness of an author's characters is not entirely *reducible* to the words on the page, for we construct out of these words a sense of a larger whole involving all those beliefs and assumptions about humankind in general that we cannot help taking for granted: what the author tells us defines the limits of character and personality. On reflexion this may seem obvious. It seems worth insisting on it formally when writing about Dickens, because in the past he has often been discussed as if his characters had some independent existence and merely dropped into the novels for a period before continuing their life elsewhere. I am not of course meaning to argue that Dickens's people are not 'drawn from life': as J. K. Jerome amusingly shows in his introduction to *Our Mutual Friend* (he was never able to regard it as 'a mere story'), they are on the contrary immediately recognisable as types of the humanity we all live among; their relationship to reality is, in general, a fairly direct one. And to many people, including Dickens himself if we can trust the preface to *David Copperfield,* they seem to have a reality similar in kind to that of our acquaintance in life, so vividly have readers apparently been enabled to visualise them. But to extract them from the books in which they stand is to do violence to the complete work of art which is the novel, in which, in the ideal case, all the elements—plot, character, symbolism, and so on—are perfectly fused to fulfil the work's total purpose, and none can exist or even be defined in isolation from the rest. Moreover the vehicle of character is always the novelist's handling of language. When Pecksniff is attempting to preside at the family gathering he begins by using commonplace effusions to refer to Old Martin, whose illness and expected death are the cause of their all being there:

> 'What I would observe is, that I think some practical means might be devised of inducing our respected—shall I say our revered—?'
> 'No!' interposed the strong-minded woman in a loud voice.

'Then I will not', said Mr. Pecksniff. 'You are quite right, my dear madam, and I appreciate and thank you for your discriminating objection—our respected relative, to dispose himself to listen to the promptings of nature, and not to the—'   MC iv

And he professes to be unable to think of the word he wants. Here is Dickens enjoying deflating the pretensions of conventional compliment (rhetorical questions do not expect answers). Yet the exchange also does much to make Pecksniff's oiliness vivid to us. And we say 'Pecksniff's oiliness' not because there was a real Pecksniff and real (or figurative) oil, but because we are concerned with the delineation of a character who will stand *within the novel* as representative of certain human characteristics (including oiliness).

Or consider another flash of wit as Dickens picks up a familiar old notion and turns it to unexpectedly rich use. The evil Carker has visited Florence Dombey while she stayed with the Skettleses, filling her with intense revulsion:

> Florence was seized with such a shudder as he went, that Sir Barnet, adopting the popular superstition, supposed somebody was passing over her grave. Mr. Carker, turning a corner, on the instant, looked back, and bowed, and disappeared, as if he rode off to the churchyard straight to do it.   D & S xxv

Suddenly the old superstition is sinisterly alive, making palpable the threat which Carker carries with him—no longer merely a notion one scarcely thinks about when it is quoted, but a clear image of the man's central character.

These two incidents seem to me typical of the way the novelist builds up an impression of his characters in the reader: they are both economical and vivid, and they are inexplicable outside their particular place in the complex structure of the novel. Though important in the delineation of character, they help to ensure that character is closely related to the developing significance of the whole, illustrating therefore the interconnectedness of character and other elements in the novel—which it is important to bear in mind when for the sake of clarity we discuss these elements separately.

Those who are fond of talking of Dickensian 'characters'

generally have at the top of their minds the eccentrics who shade off into caricature and can so easily be recognised by tricks of speech or behaviour: everyone remembers Major Bagstock's ways of referring to himself, or how Phil Squod moves round a room; and Mrs. Gamp's umbrella quickly passed into our language. It is not really a sign of strength in character-drawing that these features stick so firmly in our memory, for in doing so they are detaching themselves from their books—in which, it must be said, a good many of them belong rather by accident anyway: many such 'characters' could be translated from one novel to another with the minimum of adjustment to their circumstances. If this is so it obviously implies a loose relationship of character to theme, and even to plot, at least in the peripheries of Dickens's created world. But the looseness and peripheral incoherence are the price we pay for the copiousness of Dickens's art, for his ability to give the central activity of his novels a setting vibrant with the manifold (and sometimes distracting) comprehensiveness of life in a large and intricate community.

In fact many of his more obvious 'characters' have important roles to play near the centre of the novels, and this not simply in the essential development of the plot. Harold Skimpole in *Bleak House* is involved in the central action when he betrays Jo to Inspector Bucket; but if there were no more important use for him it would be easy to provide some other piece of machinery for getting Jo out of the house. The story as such could get on very well without him, as it could without the Jellybys and Turveydrops. Yet Skimpole is an important part of the thematic structure of the novel: where so many people are not what they seem, he is (to all but Jarndyce) a particularly transparent example of fraud, and he is representative of a particularly insiduous kind of self-centredness which makes indefinite claims on others while recognising none on itself. Unlike Mrs. Jellyby, who makes a great parade of the selfless work she is doing for others, thus giving an overweening sense of self-importance, Skimpole attains his end by professing unfitness for *any* work; both are equally careless of the real duties which they owe to those who have close claims on them.

Picture of Snow's Rents, Westminster, from Parliamentary Papers 1844.

MY MAGNIFICENT ORDER AT THE PUBLIC-HOUSE

A Phiz illustration from *David Copperfield*.

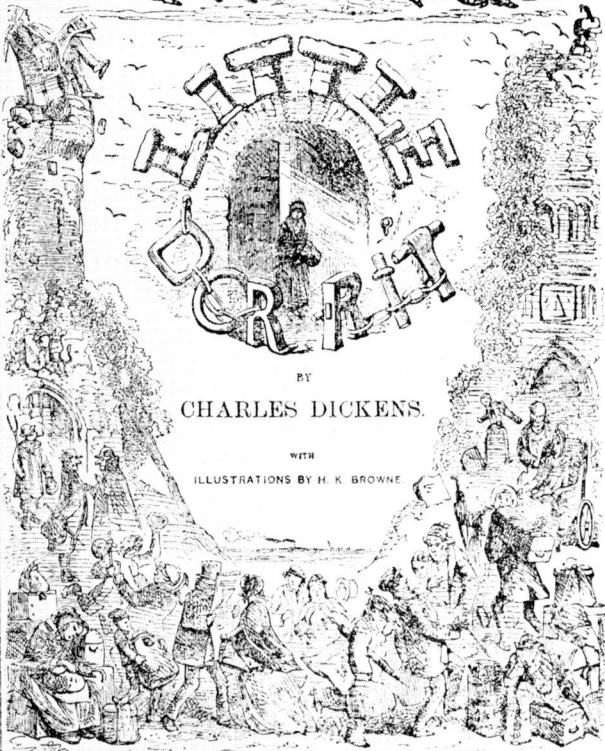

The title page of the first monthly number of *Little Dorrit*, 1855.

VIEW OF A DUST YARD.
(From a Sketch taken on the spot.)

View of a Dust Yard from Mayhew's *London Labour and the London Poor*, 1861.

Mr. Tulkinghorn presents a different case. Obviously he is essential to the plot of *Bleak House*: without his desire for power over others, especially the 'great', Lady Dedlock's story would never be uncovered. So his obsession may seem to make him a one-dimensional character with only a single defining quality, as are Skimpole and Mrs. Jellyby. But the nature of the obsession gives him a wider interest for us. He concentrates all his energies, all his attention, on a single object, and by so doing, to the neglect of all others, shows himself to be so entirely without a moral sense that he is blind to the dangers to himself that his activities lead him into. He is murdered because he is ignorant of the strength of passions which he has never felt and in consequence despises and discounts.

Dickens's study of Tulkinghorn is steady and single-minded, but wholly external. This is not in his case, any more than in Mr. Dorrit's, an inadequacy of presentation; for the workings of his mind are in essence simple, dominated as he is by his simple (though corrupt) morality. Now it would be absurd to suggest that Dickens ever reaches the psychological penetration and profundity of the greatest of George Eliot's studies—Mrs. Transome, Lydgate, Gwendolen Harleth. But from his earliest books Dickens has not been content to work only with characters who can be adequately portrayed in the manner of Tulkinghorn. Fagin, when we first see him, is shown from the improbable child's-eye view of Oliver Twist: though the narrative is third-person, we learn nothing of Fagin but what Oliver's vision sees and implies. But towards the end of the novel Oliver obviously moves away from the centre of Dickens's interest, and Fagin and Sikes are shown without intermediary. I cannot say that the agony of Sikes after the murder of Nancy strikes me as particularly convincing; but Fagin's end is another matter. The quiet intensity of the trial scene is most impressive:

> He looked up into the gallery again . . . There was one young man sketching his face in a little note-book. He wondered whether it was like, and looked on when the artist broke his pencil-point, and made another with his knife, as any idle spectator might have done.
> In the same way, when he turned his eyes towards the judge, his

mind began to busy itself with the fashion of his dress, and what it cost, and how he put it on. There was an old fat gentleman on the bench, too, who had gone out, some half an hour before, and now come back. He wondered within himself whether this man had been to get his dinner, what he had had, and where he had had it; and pursued this train of careless thought until some new object caught his eye and roused another.

Not that, all this time, his mind was, for an instant, free from one oppressive overwhelming sense of the grave that opened at his feet; it was ever present to him, but in a vague and general way, and he could not fix his thoughts upon it.   OT lii

(This particular experience, of finding it impossible to concentrate on the immediate details of a personal catastrophe, is one to which in different circumstances Dickens reverts much later: when David Copperfield hears of his mother's death, he is overcome with grief. 'And yet my thoughts were idle; not intent on the calamity that weighed upon my heart, but idly loitering near it.' (*DC,* ix)). Here surely we have an example of the imaginative power of the artist to project himself into the interior of an experience which he has not suffered in reality: we are here seeing Fagin's fear from the inside—a fear which keeps his immediate thoughts away from the one overwhelming fact, just as David's awareness of grief kept him from thinking directly about its cause.

Dickens's interest in portraying the inner workings of consciousness nevertheless remained fitful for a long time. One does not think of him as characteristically a psychological novelist. Jonas Chuzzlewit's terror after *his* murder of Montague recalls the descriptions of Sikes at Hatfield, and it is much more plausible in that we have been shown the narrow, stultified cunning which makes up so much of his mind. Martin's case in the same novel is treated so much more casually that it seems plain that Dickens has no real interest in convincing the reader of its psychological reality; and the weakness in this presentation is a characteristic one in the working out of Dicken's more solemn intentions. Richard Carstone in *Bleak House* is a more extended and perhaps ultimately damaging case in point. The gradual and steady increase of the power that the Chancery suit has over him, its effect of eating away his power of discernment with the particular result of his growing suspicion of Jarndyce: this is interesting and acceptable, despite the occasional use of the clichés of worry—dry lips and bitten fingernails—which are unsatisfactory not because worried people do not sometimes bite their nails but because these conventional accompaniments are doing duty for the real evocation of the particular mental state which is what we need. Dickens has not, as in Fagin's case, seen what the state really is like—he has simply hung out conventional signs. There are moments when the progress of Richard's derangement does seem to be seen at first hand, as when Esther reports that

> he told us, more than once, that Vholes was a good fellow, a safe fellow, a man who did what he pretended to do—a very good fellow indeed! He was so defiant about it, that it struck me he had begun to doubt Mr. Vholes. Then he threw himself on the sofa, tired out.
>
> BH lx

The rapid, spasmodic alternation of vehement energy and total exhaustion is conveyed directly by the sudden drop in the energy of the language. For the most part, however, Richard's downward career is not looked at closely enough to make us feel that this is a true tragedy: what happens to him seems largely notional, abstracted from reality. And this is confirmed by the pretentious solemnity which surrounds his death. On his deathbed his eyes are opened to the truth, the nightmare of illusion has gone, but it is now too late for him to 'begin the world':

> A smile irradiated his face, as [Ada] bent to kiss him. He slowly laid his face down upon her bosom, drew his arms closer round her neck, and with one parting sob began the world. Not this world, oh, not this! The world that sets this right.
>
> BH lxv

Obviously at this moment, if not before, Dickens goes soft, as he does at so many deathbeds. His aim now seems not to make Richard see the devastation he has caused, but so far as is possible to eliminate the pain altogether—the damage will all be 'set right' but not through any exertion of ours. So Richard's story is not a tragedy in which wisdom is purchased through suffering, but, rather, a sentimental morality, in which we are given a solemn death scene to remember the lesson by: the connexion between the two is not radical, only associative, and for this reason sentimental. This is the price of an inability to experience Richard's sufferings as something deriving from the situation he made for himself: the developing situation ought to define the sufferings that come from it, but not being well understood itself cannot provide more than an abstract. Dickens has given us a scheme instead of the recreation of a living experience.

A similar weakness repeatedly confounds his dramatic heroines and villainesses. Of the latter Miss Dartle (*David Copperfield*) seems to me demonstrably a literary contrivance: her viciousness towards Emily and her father can be explained fairly enough as a sublimated envy, arising out of her thwarted love for Steerforth, but Dickens seems in two minds about her. When in Chapter xx she is informed by Steerforth that the poor are really quite insensitive, her reply seems heavily ironic, not simply on Dickens's part but as intended to imply that she is speaking ironically:

> 'Well, I don't know, now, when I have been better pleased than to hear that. It's so consoling! It's such a delight to know that, when they suffer, they don't feel! Sometimes I have been quite uneasy for that sort of people; but now I shall just dismiss the idea of them altogether. Live and learn. I had my doubts, I confess, but now they're cleared up. I didn't know, and now I do know, and that shows the advantage of asking—don't it?'

The jaunty assumption of having just been through a kind of educational process seems impossible to speak without mockery in the voice. Yet later, when David brings Mr. Peggotty to interview Mrs. Steerforth after the elopement (Chapter xxxii), there can be no doubt that Miss Dartle has absorbed Steerforth's contemptuous attitude and turned it into vituperative scorn. The intensely melodramatic scene in which she finally tracks Emily down and turns on her is blatantly stagey. Because of the first-person narrative we have to accept David standing in the wings watching and listening to what is presumably meant to be an outburst from someone whose obsession has passed beyond the bounds of madness. Mr. Peggotty's arrival is obviously held back so that there can be as much of it as possible.

> 'Listen to what I say! . . . and reserve your false arts for your dupes. Do you hope to move *me* by your tears? No more than you could charm me by your smiles, you purchased slave.' DC 1

And so on. Dickens has, as elsewhere, given us something specious that can only be taken for an expression of passion by those who think and feel in clichés—all stage heroics and false airs—and he has not seen that this will not do, because he has not bothered to understand what might really be the passion of someone in Miss Dartle's place.

By the time he created Miss Wade in *Little Dorrit,* he really knew what it was about. Her history is less a history than a self-exposure—of one who is obsessed with the idea that she can never be loved and is therefore being patronised and despised by all who show generosity or just friendliness towards her. When she is in service as a governess the delicacy that her mistress constantly shows, Miss Wade 'knows' to be 'her way of petting the knowledge that she was my mistress, and might have behaved differently to her servant if it had been her fancy'. She becomes the counterpart of Henry Gowan, with his cynical assumption that everyone is false who does not admit to acting out of selfish motives. Miss Wade says often that she 'saw directly' or 'fully understood' what people were up to—which means that she had the obsessive's power to torture everything into evidence for her own distorted view of life: since she has never felt any disinterested or generous impulse in herself, she denies that it can exist in anyone; all is cunning and artifice, and 'love' means only a fierce possessiveness, a desire for power over the 'beloved'. Hence she taunts Tattycoram for being dependent on her, for does this not show the weakness of subservience to which Miss Wade has never yielded? And likewise she instinctively distrusts her as well in that she will not be made quite tame and submissive, and this is a sign of the limits of Miss Wade's own power. Dickens's insight is remarkably keen and sure here: he does not really give us, as he seems to offer, the origin of Miss Wade's self-destructive obsession, but the neurosis itself is seen with great clarity and related with great steadiness of purpose. How close, we see, cynicism is to sentimentality: sentimentality implies an arbitrary or misplaced association of feeling with object or behaviour; cynicism, the habitual disparagement of motive, involves the *dislocation* of feeling from action and the assumption of arbitrary motive in its stead.

Dickens seems to me to show a rare detachment and objectivity in the portrait of Miss Wade: he has a human fact very clearly in front of him and does not allow himself to be distracted from a steady facing of it. In short he knows exactly what he is talking about. With his dramatic heroines one cannot have the same confidence. There are those, like Agnes Wickfield, Little Dorrit, Lizzie Hexam, who are plainly idealised. By this I mean not simply that they are set upon a pedestal and displayed as an ideal human example (a point which is patent in Agnes's case and only slightly less obvious in Little Dorrit's), but also that the act of idealising them prevents Dickens's putting a simulacrum of the real before us, prevents indeed his seeing them as real. It is not cynical to observe that the ideal is not often realised in humanity with much constancy; but that is no objection if an artist can make us accept it on occasion: there can be no objection of this kind against Cordelia. But in these heroines of Dickens there is something contradictory. It cannot be a wholly consistent transformation of the ideal into the real which gives rise to such smugness and self-satisfaction. Not that Agnes or Little Dorrit is shown to us as self-satisfied; but it is obviously a point for self-congratulation in David that he all along appreciates how unapproachably perfect Agnes is. And when we come to Esther Summerson it is only by the most transparent and factitious artifice that we avoid (so far as we do) open self-admiration; for instead of Esther's telling us herself how wonderful she is, Dickens arranges for Ada or others to do it for her while Esther simpers in the background. Furthermore it must also be something of a limitation on the ideal that it is so lacking in spirit, that only by further artifice can these heroines be engineered into taking any action on their own at all: meekness is not a virtue when it is really spinelessness. Florence Dombey seems to me more acceptable as what Dickens intends her for, because she does not, as Esther does, pretend that she does not suffer, and there comes a point at which she cannot bear any more. Even Lizzie's impassiveness is not proof against a vigorous dislike of Bradley Headstone and a resentment of his and Charley's attempts to bully and force her.

There is certainly more action from another kind of Dickensian heroine, who is far from being ideal: the energy with which Edith Dombey and eventually Lady Dedlock act derives indeed in part from what Dickens sees as the less than admirable side of their natures and so is itself implicitly condemned. Lady Dedlock finds peace only in death, but the feverish energy of what comes just before is associated with her long unexpiated 'crime'. Just so, she can once stir herself into activity to tell Esther the truth. But then, alas, what do we get?

> 'My child, my child! . . . For the last time! These kisses for the last time! These arms upon my neck for the last time! We shall meet no more. To hope to do what I seek to do, I must be what I have been so long. Such is my reward and doom. If you hear of Lady Dedlock, brilliant, prosperous, and flattered, think of your wretched mother, conscience-stricken, underneath that mask! Think that the reality is in her suffering, in her useless remorse, in her murdering within her breast the only love and truth of which it is capable! And then forgive her, if you can; and cry to Heaven to forgive her, which it never can!'   BH xxxvi

The explanation of this—it cannot be called an excuse—must be a terror of the power of the sexual impulse (it is characteristic of Dickens that he should present Esther's birth as what had to be forgiven rather than her mother's partly self-imposed avoidance of her: would not a real Esther suspect or resent a torrent of feeling from one who has kept away so long?). There is a perverse delight in the thrilled heroism of this stuff—the sense of daring, the wickedness that is unforgivable—which is the more distasteful in that Lady Dedlock's end, as well as those of Jo and Richard are suffused with a glow of sentimental optimism about 'forgiveness' and expiation. The scene is written up in strong words and false lights, to give a sense of exciting emotion which at the same time we know is tainted with shame: we are, that is, invited to share the luxury of indulging and condemning the evil at the same time. But the entire situation of Lady Dedlock is melodramatised to the point of unintended caricature: Dickens seems so determined that the crime should be worked out that he makes his heroine responsible for a grotesquely exaggerated self-condemnation and ultimately for the convulsive action which leads to her death. She is imprisoned within the novelist's conception of the moral role she has to play (he cannot allow her to be forgiven on this earth, which gives a grotesque irony to Sir Leicester's nobility towards her); this has prevented his coming close enough to her to see the truth, and so he contents himself with the outward conventional trappings of emotion.

In Bradley Headstone in *Our Mutual Friend,* Dickens gives us his most detailed and striking inner study of obsession, which differs from that of Miss Wade not only in length but in that we watch his whole progress. It is impossible to discuss Bradley Headstone except in connexion with Eugene Wrayburn: his whole being in the book is determined by his passion for Lizzie and his consequent hatred for Eugene. This may seem to make the study a very superficial one. In the early presentation of Headstone, there is, in such a detail as his repeatedly biting his finger, what may seem at first the same contentment with clichés of emotional expression that I have complained of in Lady Dedlock. But is this the same?

> Mr. Bradley Headstone, highly certificated stipendiary schoolmaster, drew his right forefinger through one of the buttonholes of the boy's coat, and looked at it attentively. 'I hope your sister may be good company for you?'
> 'Why do you doubt it, Mr. Headstone?'
> 'I did not say I doubted it.'
> 'No, sir; you didn't say so.'
> Bradley Headstone looked at his finger again, took it out of the buttonhole and looked at it closer, bit the side of it and looked at it again. OMF xviii

This seems to me, in the close relating of detail of action and speech, very keenly observed: the detail is not applied to a ready-made conception, it defines the individual. And though there is one bad moment in the scene of the meeting between Headstone and Wrayburn in the Temple—when Headstone apostrophises himself in a melodramatic gesture which is not his own—the scene as a whole goes well. What Dickens sees here is that Headstone is a man obsessed with class, with his own rise to a social position above that of his birth; and his obsession makes him see everyone with whom he is in contact as equally, though from hostile points of view, concerned with it. When Wrayburn suggests unsympathetically that Headstone would like to be Lizzie's schoolmaster as well as Charley's, he adds that it is

'a natural ambition enough. . . . The sister . . . is so very different from all the associations to which she has been used, and from all the low obscure people about her, that it is a very natural ambition.'

'Do you throw my obscurity in my teeth, Mr. Wrayburn?'

'That can hardly be, for I know nothing concerning it, School-master, and seek to know nothing.'

'You reproach me with my origin', said Bradley Headstone; 'you cast insinuations at my bringing-up. But I tell you, sir, I have worked my way onward, out of both and in spite of both, and have a right to be considered a better man than you, with better reasons for being proud.'   OMF xxiii

In the man obsessed with his origin and his rise from it, it seems to need permanent vigilance to stay in the position so laboriously attained. Wrayburn's easy confidence of *his* position (of which he is not consciously aware) must in itself *seem* contemptuous to the man who cannot be thus at his ease; and in this scene no reader can feel comfortable at Wrayburn's satisfaction in his own suavity and self-control. It has already something of cruelty in it. Yet Headstone's passion is coloured by his self-absorption, and the scene is no comfort either to those sentimentalists who find a special virtue in the mere fact of mean birth.

Headstone's passion for Lizzie is really an extension of his concern with his own rise and status. And he sees *her* as an extension of himself:

'The sister . . . suffers under no reproach that repels a man of un-impeachable character, who has made for himself every step of his way in life, from placing her in his own station. I will not say raising her to his own station; I say, placing her in it. The sister labours under no reproach, unless she should unfortunately make it for her-self. When such a man is not deterred from regarding her as his equal, and when he has convinced himself that there is no blemish on her, I think the fact must be taken to be pretty expressive.'

OMF xxxi

The expression may remind one momentarily of Bounderby; yet the effect in context is quite different. Obviously there is an arrogance in Headstone that he should set himself up as Lizzie's judge; but what one is most conscious of is the pathetic anxiety lest he do anything, by word or deed, to put his 'station' at risk. Headstone is not a specially attractive figure, and his violent attempt to bully Lizzie into accepting him as her lover alienates him permanently from the reader's main sympathies. Yet even this—even the 'dark look of hatred and revenge' which accom-panies his extreme outburst of jealousy towards Wrayburn—do not eliminate the pathos of his plight. What above all charac-terises his approach to Lizzie is his habit of self-dramatisation and self-pity; but though these are unappealing emotions to the out-sider they do not thereby become any the less painful, and Lizzie 'compassionated the bitter struggle he could not conceal, almost as much as she was repelled and alarmed by it' (xxxii). When he exclaims to her that she could draw him to fire, to water, to the gallows, and so forth, he is of course indulging in melodramatic commonplaces; but it is the effect of his intense self-absorption to make him think or express himself thus; an overwhelming self-consuming passion takes away the possibility of detachment and discrimination. His love for Lizzie and loathing for Wray-burn are simply different and related expressions of his own pas-sionate concern with himself. Though Lizzie remains the nominal motive of his vindictive pursuit, she is almost forgotten in the outcome: the hatred feeds on itself, and Wrayburn is now the central, perhaps the only, object of his passion. His violently spasmodic activity has always been governed by negative, in-turned emotion; and self-love is now expressing itself as envy unalloyed by any gloss of positive feeling.

It is not an attractive picture; yet our sympathy is never totally removed from him, partly because he is throughout the chief sufferer from his own feelings and actions, partly because Dickens allows us no very rosy view of Wrayburn. If Headstone is a victim of his own passion, Wrayburn takes a vindictive delight in goading him to give the passion rein, until hunter and hunted change places. Now as the passion of the self-absorbed man is self-destructive, so the hunt which he engages in becomes inverted, he is now the object of the hunt, yet he remains the moving cause. The power of the metaphor is the greater in that his hunting of Wrayburn is itself a natural extension of his previous behaviour; the hunting is inescapably part of the real story (reaching a climax in the assault by the river), advancing at once the development of the action and our moral understanding of it. Here is Headstone when Wrayburn and Lightwood finally come face to face with him at the end of Chapter xliii:

> Looking like the hunted, and not the hunter, baffled, worn, with the exhaustion of deferred hope and consuming hate and anger in his face, white-lipped, wild-eyed, draggle-haired, seamed with jealousy and anger, and torturing himself with the conviction that he showed it all and they exulted in it, he went by them in the dark, like a haggard head suspended in the air: so completely did the force of his expression cancel his figure.

His wretchedness is inescapable and painful; but Dickens will not allow it to conceal the other aspect of the truth: his face was 'seamed with jealousy and anger', and then the real heart of his frustrated rage is shown—'the conviction that he showed it all and they exulted in it'. Dickens keeps effect and cause in close connexion, and makes the cause explicit. And the final astonishing image clinches the concentration of agony and hatred where both express themselves—the rest is, as it were, of no account.

(vi) PLOTTING

A good deal has incidentally been said about the role and nature of the plot during the discussion of other elements of Dickens's fiction and more will be said later in examinations of particular novels. Here, still talking about *Our Mutual Friend,* I wish to look at the main plot, which I believe to be a total failure, turning a potentially great novel into one which is only intermittently satisfying. (It is proper to admit at the start that this is probably a minority view and that to some readers *Our Mutual Friend* is Dickens's finest achievement.) The failure, however, is extremely interesting and will help to establish certain grounds for discrimination in discovering the relation of his plots and characters to what Arnold Kettle, rather unfortunately I think, calls Dickens's moral patterns (see his essay in *Dickens and the Twentieth Century*). Unfortunately because it suggests that Dickens, at any rate in his later work, began with a carefully elaborated moral schema for which he then devised an appropriate story to dramatise or illustrate it. Now there is clear evidence in the mass of material that has survived relating to the composition of Dickens's novels that this 'moral pattern' was never set until the book was well under way; that, as with any good novelist, his characters and story, once partially created, began to act as it were of themselves, their actions arising out of the definitions of personality and situation which Dickens made for them. This is not to say that Dickens was or could have been unaware of the moral significance of the wider relationships in which his people move; but that he knew instinctively that there would be an artistic corruption in imposing a pattern which did not grow out of the living characters he had created; moreover the moral purpose itself would be thwarted. The novelist must find his morality in the life that he sees, records and creates.

Now I have given instances where just this kind of moral imposition seems to have happened; it is certainly possible to construct a moral pattern which makes sense of the apparently incoherent structure of *Our Mutual Friend.* My contention is, however, that this can only be done through a kind of violence both to our moral sensibilities and to our sense of fact. The main plot of the book—the story centring on the relationship between John Harmon and Bella Wilfer—is a confection of two age-old and well-tried stories. The first is that of the young couple whose future is parentally settled before they meet, who each react by falling in love with the one who eventually turns out to be in fact the chosen mate. The second is that of the rich man who wants to be loved for himself alone and not for his money, and so feigns poverty to test the true inclinations of his intended bride. These two fairy-tale plots are varied and elaborated by Dickens: thus Bella is the only one of the two young people who does not know who the other really is, and she is by no means steadfastly disinterested: much of the action in fact turns not on testing her, but on changing or making her discover her essential nature. Unlike the simpler versions of the first plot, therefore, the deception practised on Bella is a one-sided matter; and it changes character as the story develops. Once Harmon in his guise of impecunious secretary has been spurned by Bella, there must be a change of direction: this spurning, we must be led to see, did not come out of Bella's true heart, but was a superficial and hasty response in circumstances she had not yet learnt to understand. Now up to this point Rokesmith's real identity has been concealed from everyone else in the book; and so far as the reader is concerned it continues to be his secret and his alone, for he has been shown how things really are only by the patently clumsy device of the soliloquy in Chapter xxx, though he is likely (as he is meant) to have guessed the essential truth before. From now on the deception of Bella becomes more complex, and for the first time perhaps Dickens takes pains to deliberately deceive the reader as well. This double deception is managed with much skill, though not always with complete artistic honesty. The gradual change in Mr. Boffin is seen largely through Bella's eyes; and as she watches him getting more and more miserly and spiteful, she likewise sees the growing anxiety in Mrs. Boffin and irritation and bitterness in Rokesmith. The reader also sees Boffin in his new character with Silas Wegg at the Bower, with Mr. Venus in his workshop, and most significantly at least once by himself, when he walks home after striking his bargain with Venus:

'Now I wonder', he meditated as he went along, nursing his

stick, 'whether it can be, that Venus is setting himself to get the better of Wegg? Whether it can be, that he means, when I have bought Wegg out, to have me all to himself and to pick me clean to the bones?'

It was a cunning and suspicious idea, quite in the way of his school of Misers, and he looked very cunning and suspicious as he went jogging through the streets. xlvii

This passage is not inconsistent with the discovery so much later that Boffin's miserliness is all a pretence; and there are occasions—for example, that of his arrival at the Bower with the first batch of miserly biographies (Chapter xxxix)—when with the hindsight of later knowledge we can spot some clues which point to the truth. Yet I am certain that Dickens means the reader to be as comprehensively deceived as Bella: it is not only Bella who sees Mr. Boffin's radiant face in Chapter lxiii with astonishment. Everything we have read up to this point about him suggests that he was really being corrupted by his money: now we learn that it was all an elaborate pretence. Why should Dickens play this trick on us? Granted it is essential to Dickens's plan that Bella should be thoroughly taken in, or, since that begs the question, thoroughly convinced that Boffin has gone to the bad; why nevertheless does he give him this retrospective exculpation? Humphry House (*The Dickens World,* Chapter vi) plausibly suggests that Dickens may himself have been taken in at first:

the episode of the miserhood is so convincingly done that one is tempted to wonder whether Dickens did not mean it to be genuine and only changed his mind towards the end.

External evidence does not support this view. But if House is right, Dickens reprieved Boffin much as he had earlier reprieved Walter Gay; only here the effect on the novel is more serious. For it leads us to question what one may call the engineering of this central aspect of the book, and, through that, its morality.

It is important not to get two separate but related themes confused. That the love of money is the root of all evil is a theme that Dickens never tired of: Bella's main danger is that her understandable desire to get away from the squalid narrowness of her poor home (the suffocating effect of which is extremely vivid) will turn to cupidity and that she will sacrifice for money things that matter more, and matter more *to her*. Cupidity is indeed rife in the novel—at its extreme in Fledgby, who is a miser like Boffin's Dancers and Blackberry Jones and corrupts others into his service, in Riderhood who is a vicious blackmailer and Silas Wegg who is a blustering and incompetent one. But the possession of money does not in itself bring evil: indeed riches will be Bella's ultimate reward for her generous heart and unquestioning loyalty to John. Dickens's purpose, therefore (John's and Boffin's as well), in the elaborate scheme of deception is not so much to demonstrate the inevitable corrupting power of money, but to make Bella come to a realisation and decision about what really matters to her most. Nevertheless the success of the scheme depends vitally on the convincingness of the fraud: if Boffin's decline into miserliness is not a good imitation of the real thing, it will not work—Bella must be made to see at close hand what happens if you put money first, for even the admirable Boffin is corruptible. But the trouble is that he is not. The whole performance is only a parade, a complicated piece of fictional machinery, the operation and progress of which are not interesting in themselves, for they have no reality (we cannot be interested in the change in Boffin, for there is no change in him), machinery whose sole function *inside the plot* is to trick Bella into a situation where she at last realises her true nature. But Dickens cannot resist tricking the reader too. The reader, who knows a lot about Bella by this time, has seen her in conversation with her cheerful and long-suffering father and knows that her cupidity is only skin-deep, doubtless expects her to be brought round by this frighteningly close example of the danger of money in the foreground of her view of human affairs. But he himself must react in a parallel way—Boffin's downward career is, for so large a part of the book, the central demonstration of money's corrupting power; but the moral significance of this is eliminated when the corruption is shown to be bogus. It is no good making out a lesson that money corrupts when the whole point of the end of the story is that it has not corrupted Boffin. What perhaps has happened is that Dickens cannot really allow the reader to see that Bella is being fooled (for this would give the game away and make the outcome of the story too easily foreseen) and therefore runs the greater risk that the reader will in the end feel cheated himself. But perhaps Dickens really did change his mind: that sounds like a considerable failure of nerve, as if he could not bear his beloved Boffin to come into real danger, and so allowed the book's moral centre to become hollow and ineffectual.

It will be replied that since the trick works, since it does bring Bella to her true senses, it is thereby justified and these complaints are beside the point. But in the first place can we believe that the trick does or could really work? Is it, as a whole, plausible? To say it is involves us in accepting that not only Boffin himself, but John Harmon and Mrs. Boffin as well, are consummate actors in a kind of impromptu drama that continually threatens to take them by surprise. It is simply not credible that these three should be so expert in this kind of deception that for months they can so completely fool an intelligent girl living at close quarters with all of them. So the performance tells either against Bella's intelligence or against the reality of this whole large part of the plot. It seems to me that the convincingness of Dickens's narrative is such that we could only believe in it if Boffin, and hence the other two as well, were not pretending. Working on such an ample scale, Dickens is obliged to reveal a great deal of the machinery of his plot, and it is precisely the machinery which will least bear direct observation. The trick has only been made to work by being made utterly impossible.

But perhaps even more unfortunate than the strain this imposes on our credulity is the strain it surely ought to impose on our moral sensibility. When all is revealed to her, Bella can only think of her own unworthiness:

> 'You said, my pretty', Mrs. Boffin reminded Bella, 'that there was one other thing you couldn't understand.'
> 'Oh yes!' cried Bella, covering her face with her hands; 'but that I never shall be able to understand as long as I live. It is how John could love me so when I so little deserved it, and how you, Mr. and Mrs. Boffin, could be so forgetful of yourselves, and take such pains

> and trouble to make me a little better, and after all to help him to so
> unworthy a wife. But I am very, very grateful.'   lxiii

Dickens warmly endorses her attitude by waving away, almost as
Podsnap would, John's explanation of his deception of her. Yet
she has been the victim of a long-drawn-out moral imposture,
during the course of which her husband has concealed his
identity from her (an identity in which she had after all a peculiar
interest) and led her on by a series of temptations to demonstrate
her loyalty to him; and the whole point, as she so ingenuously
reveals, was to 'make her better'! Who are these people that they
should set themselves up as her moral superiors and mentors, and
engineer their course of improvement by means of a complicated
and heartless fraud that seems to last for at least two years of her
life? Though Bella may feel there is nothing to forgive, the
reader cannot be so easily satisfied.

The painfulness of this moral engineering comes out especially
clearly when one thinks of the case of Silas Wegg, who is Bella's
antithesis, and on whom a rather similar trick is played, though
not of course with any high intention: no one has any idea of
making Silas Wegg better, and everyone is delighted when he
gets his comeuppance at the end. Dickens can rely on the reader's
relishing Silas Wegg's being paid out in his own coin, because
he has been so thoroughly mean himself; yet as House remarks
(*loc. cit.*), Boffin has behaved to him 'rather like mistresses who
leave half-crowns in corners hoping the servants will steal them'.
He too has been tested by a deception (the same deception), and,
having comprehensively failed, is dispatched with a good deal of
gusto and enjoyment, rather as Mr. Guppy had been (see *BH,*
lxiv): certainly we are to waste no tears on him. Is this what
would have happened to Bella if she had not come out strong at
the right moment? But of course the question is absurd: she
could not have failed to. And this fact demonstrates the essentially
artificial and confected nature of the whole elaborate business.

There is one final issue of some note which arises in similar
forms in several other novels and which makes one question the
completeness of Dickens's moral perception. Bella passes her test
triumphantly, and her reward is precisely the riches that she

earlier renounced when they were opposed to integrity and decency. Doubtless there is poetic justice in this—that what she gave up for love should come back to her with love. But from the point of view of the reader entering fully into the rightness of Bella's explosion against Mr. Boffin in Chapter xlviii, she is simply being allowed to have her cake and eat it. Not only does the moral seem to be that uprightness brings its own reward in the goods of this world; but she is the occasion by which the reader can vicariously enjoy both the sense of the uprightness of virtue withstanding or conquering temptation on its own account, and the comfort of virtue recognised by a handsome share in the world's treasure. So too, more offensively, David Copperfield, Esther Summerson and Nicholas Nickleby are each given the luxury of a self-sacrifice of which they take all possible advantage to display their nobility before the reader who knows perfectly well that in the next chapter or the next but one it is all going to be shown up as a charade. (Each, that is, is in the beautifully comfortable position of being heroically self-sacrificing and losing nothing by it.) The rewards of Florence and Bella are less objectionable than those of Esther and Nicholas, partly because the two girls do not make a dramatic case of their selflessness; but taking all five novels together, one can hardly avoid the conclusion that Dickens wishes us to learn that one of the great merits of being virtuous is that it enables one to get what one wants with an easy conscience. In this of course he is not alone.

Finally, it seems impossible to devise any satisfactory explanation of why the two plots are together in the same book. If anything makes a united novel of *Our Mutual Friend* the two great generating images should—the river and the dust. Both get their special significance from their association with London: it is in London that the river becomes corrupted, and only in London can one make money out of collecting dirt. But Dickens makes no effort to express directly a connexion between the images: their working, not altogether very impressive when taken singly, is entirely inert in conjunction. Those writers who have claimed to discover a grandiose moral scheme in the book of which the images are a forceful and poignant expression have largely constructed the patterns out of what they think the images ought to present and define. It is a remarkable fact that in this book which—perhaps more than any other Dickens novel —is so eminently of London, though the very individual character of the London dockland is rendered with an extraordinary vividness which inescapably comes from one who knows it most intimately, the rest of the city makes little impact. Even the area where the Wilfers live, which must have been like the Dickenses' part of Camden Town, has not in itself much presence (we always go inside the house pretty quickly): compare it with the description of the Carkers' house in *Dombey and Son*, Chapter xxxiii. In *Our Mutual Friend* London, apart from the dockland, is a mere device for loosely locating scenes that have to take place somewhere (for after all anything may happen in London). The notable flatness of the descriptions virtually throughout, the inertness of the images, the laborious elaboration of plots that have no essential reason for lying together—these, though they do not (in view of the excellences already discussed) justify, go some way to explain James's contention that *Our Mutual Friend* 'is poor with the poverty of permanent exhaustion', a piece of work rather from the 'manufacturer of fictions' than from the genuine artist.

In fact Dickens's plots rather often seem the work of a manufacturer of fictions. *Hard Times* and *Great Expectations* are the clearest exceptions, in which not only are the plots coherently and consistently developed, retaining their own inner logic, but they do so because they are the natural expression of a compelling and single-minded interest in their author: plot and theme are consummately fused. Not all the other novels (especially not the earlier ones) suffer from the laborious contrivances by which two naturally unconnected stories are yoked together. But Dickens's plots tend undeniably to be ramshackle, and are often conceived not as smoothly developing sequences of events interesting in themselves in relation to one another, but as bridges connecting great static scenes. The plot of *Pickwick* is the barest excuse for moving from one episode to another. Whatever the main theme of *Martin Chuzzlewit* may be thought to be, it certainly does not *impose* the trip to America, which is there partly perhaps for commercial reasons, but also because Dickens had some strong feelings about the United States which he urgently wanted to get off his chest, or, in novelistic terms, because he had his eye on certain grand scenes for which his plot had to provide an opening and occasion. What one remembers chiefly from the earlier novels are the great set pieces—Oliver Twist asking for more; the murder of Nancy and Fagin's trial; Quilp's tea-party in the summer-house; the gathering of the Chuzzlewits, the gobbling of food, the exposure of Pecksniff; the great storm at Yarmouth and Micawber's letter from Australia. Dickens enjoys a great scene, and especially one in which, near the end of a novel, frauds are unmasked, tricksters are caught out and mysteries cleared away. The scenes can be richly dramatic—Mr. Dorrit's speech at Mrs. Merdle's dinner-party is perhaps the most striking—but they can be little more than an opportunity for everyone to get his own back against a character who has had his way too long (for example the exposures of Mr. Bumble, Mr. Pecksniff and Silas Wegg): here one sees the moral schema showing through too prominently, and the great length of some of these scenes is a sign that there is too much slack in its working out. If one compares the family gathering of the Chuzzlewits at Pecksniff's house with that of old Peter Featherstone's relatives in *Middlemarch* (where similarly they are greedily awaiting the expected death of a rich relative), one sees the difference between a scene which is there essentially for its own comedy and keeps going by its own impetus, and one whose sinister quality (and after all the occasion and the sentiments expressed or implied *are* sinister) enlarges our understanding of the complex of impulses by which people settle their moral behaviour. Everyone can see that Dickens very often prolongs a scene for its own sake, because he enjoys it or enjoys tantalising his readers or his characters (see Clennam and John Chivery in *Little Dorrit* II, xxxvii); and he can equally well introduce one for its own sake (see the hilarious comedy of Dr. Blimber trying to make an impressive speech—*Dombey and Son,* xii).

The construction of Dickens's novels is not only looser than that of George Eliot's, with a great deal of room in which to move, it is also more often a matter of implication. As late as *Our Mutual Friend*, the part played by Podsnap in the *plot* is marginal; yet he represents and expresses a moral and social attitude that the novel could not do without—the place of this in relation to the rest must largely be inferred by the reader. Furthermore before the novels of the 1850s Dickens had hardly mastered the art of making a story that appears both unified and natural. The plot of *Martin Chuzzlewit* is lumpish and convulsive, that of *David Copperfield* a shapeless pile of remembered bits and pieces forced into a continuous story by melodramatic invention. Even *Dombey and Son*, so much finer a book than either of these, moves onward less like a broad stream than a series of wide lakes joined by sluggish and irregular rivulets—the lengths of somewhat muddy story-spinning which bring one to the next great expansive scene. Moreover there is serious dislocation about a third of the way through, following Paul's death. Up to this point, the story has developed fairly steadily the theme of the unhappy effects of Mr. Dombey's perverted pride through the contrasts of the way in which he treats his two children and between their natural affection and the frigid mechanism into which he turns all human relations. With Paul's death a climax and something of a conclusion have been reached, and there is rather obviously a period of marking time while the plot is wound up again. A good deal of impetus is thus lost, and the relation between Florence and Mr. Dombey which must bear the weight of the transition from one part of the novel to the other is of its nature hardly powerful enough. So, unlike some of the later books in which two parallel plots attempt to realise different aspects of the same theme, *Dombey and Son* has two consecutive plots, the link between which Dickens imperfectly manages.

(vii) MYSTERY, COINCIDENCE AND MELODRAMA

Much heavy weather has been made of Dickens's frequent use of mystery and coincidence in the working out of his enormously elaborate plots. This love of incorporating the strange and unexpected into the everyday Dickens shared with many other 19th-century writers, and his coincidences are not in themselves more extravagant than Charlotte Brontë's, or even George Eliot's, though his love of mystery links his serious novels with the boyish brashness which he never entirely left behind. It is not quite enough to dismiss a modern distrust of such devices by pointing out that strange coincidences do happen in real life. So they do: as Aristotle remarked, it is probable that many improbable things will happen. But it is the serious novelist's job not just to tease his readers with mystery and neat contrivance, but to make them feel a sense of inevitable rightness about whatever means he uses to bring the novel into coherence, both in plot and theme. Of course the coincidences in *Nicholas Nickleby* and *Little Dorrit* and *Great Expectations* do make one stretch one's eyes; yet they are not really serious distractions so long as one does not treat them too solemnly. Perhaps *Hard Times* and *Our Mutual Friend* are the better for being relatively free of coincidence; but the deliberate use of coincidence is only really damaging when it affects the truth and sincerity of the author's report on experience, when, that is, it shows him cooking the facts in order to fit them to a predetermined moral framework of his own. The plot of *Great Expectations*—the whole possibility of Pip's self-delusion—hangs on the coincidence of Jaggers being Magwitch's lawyer as well as Miss Havisham's; but there is really no harm in that: indeed there is virtue, for it is the ordinariness of it (Jaggers is a well-known lawyer with a high and particular reputation) which enables Dickens to show how willingly Pip deceives himself into believing what he wants to. The resolution of the central theme by means of the discovery that Magwitch is Estella's father obviously involves a more extreme use of coincidence: the chances, one may say, are against things turning out so, though Dickens goes to some pains to make it as plausible as he can. Now the point of the coincidence is of course that Pip finally learns that the girl whom he worshipped as a 'lady' and for whom he abandoned Joe and Biddy turns out to be as tarnished in her origin as is the money which he has regarded as being somehow virtuous when he thought it came from the genteel Miss Havisham but spurns as corrupt when he knows its connexion with Magwitch the criminal (see pp. 182–3). The essential point is that the coincidence does not force a moral understanding on to Pip, who has already reached this through his discovery of where his money has come from and his subsequent coming to see Magwitch as a human being to be loved and pitied, not a member of a class to be shunned. The truth about Estella's birth makes a concluding ironic comment on the extent and nature of Pip's wilfulness and folly.

Moreover the fact of the coincidence is presented to both reader and characters directly and without fuss: there is no irritating build-up of deceptive mystery such as adds a somewhat childish element of suspense to *Bleak House,* when Dickens deliberately leads us on to believing that it is Lady Dedlock who has murdered Tulkinghorn (liii and liv), or as makes a pointless diversion near the end of *Martin Chuzzlewit,* when Martin accuses Tom of treachery: the factitiousness of this example is plain to see, for when Tom reasonably asks Martin to say what his accusation is, Martin answers 'Why should I? You could not know it the better for my dwelling on it' and sweeps off (l)—a barefaced device to beat up and maintain a little mystery for the flagging conclusion to the story.

All these cases of coincidence and mystery so far mentioned are at worst characteristic minor blemishes. Coincidence becomes a major vice when a moral pattern is made to depend on a coincidence which is essentially foreign to the nature of the material of the story. The extreme example is *Oliver Twist.* Most readers have felt that Oliver is inconceivable as a product of the workhouse. Though Dickens seems to believe in the protective power of some kind of hereditary goodness which keeps Oliver innocent in the presence of so much contamination, he has even so caught himself in a contradiction. For the main point of his attack on the treatment of children in workhouses is its permanently harmful effect; and Oliver shows that it has none such on him. But worse: Oliver himself is made to perform two contradictory functions. He must be both the example of the brutal way the middle class (or those in authority) treat the poor,

95

and the example (since he turns out to be of gentle birth) of how the criminal class attempt to corrupt the godly. Arguably Dickens changes direction or interest in mid-book, and Oliver is little more than a peg on which to hang two kinds of social melodrama. He only manages to save Dickens's somewhat dubious moral purpose by having the course of his life twisted to fit extravagant coincidences that are forced on to a situation that will not bear them. The invention of Oliver and his story is something of an imposture on Dickens's part.

Sometimes Dickens tries to make us believe (and seems to believe himself) that mystery and coincidence are the sign of something almost sacred and certainly ineffable in the way the world is made. When Esther sees Lady Dedlock for the first time she has palpitations:

> Shall I ever forget the rapid beating of my heart, occasioned by the look I met as I stood up? Shall I ever forget the manner in which those handsome, proud eyes seemed to spring out of their languor, and to hold mine? . . . very strangely, there was something quickened within me. . . .   BH xviii

This is partly a plant for the reader, setting him guessing about revelations and surprises to come. But the thrilled rhetoric tells us that for Dickens and for Esther it is more than that: we are supposed to sense a mystical communication between mother and daughter, a kind of electric discharge across the physical and social distance that divides them. Yet the language is so stagey and inflated that it is plainly all a fraud: Dickens is simply making wild motions towards something that he cannot make palpable because he does not know what he is talking about. One cannot feel that he is even very much interested in what Esther's real sensations at such a moment would be. She has become a merely notional bearer of a thrill that has been manufactured inside Dickens himself. That so many of his climaxes have the sensational character which his rhetorical assertiveness insists on is plain indication that at these moments of truth Dickens, overwhelmed by the solemnity of his own feelings, is merely gesturing towards the particular, keeping no true hold on the real.

Even Louisa's return to Mr. Gradgrind (*HT*, xxviii) is somewhat spoiled when she strikes verbal attitudes. If the point were that she is the kind of girl who substitutes gesture for the true expression of feeling, this would be all right. But she is not; and Dickens, by giving us stage gestures conventionally associated with feeling, instead of the natural expression of feeling, has either falsified his character for the moment or shown that he is inattentive to truth.

Such gestures we are inclined to call melodramatic in that they make violent and obvious appeal to the emotions ungrounded in any presented experience. The love of melodrama and heroics always gets in the way of really seeing and telling the truth: because Dickens sees Lady Dedlock as the heroine-villainess of a stage melodrama he sees her as making only gestures appropriate to the part—she thinks in nothing but ciphers, and there is a hole in the book where her real agony ought to be. The climax of all the revelations about the Clennam family in *Little Dorrit* has parallel dangers: for the revelation of the heart of Mrs. Clennam's spiritual disease, which is a superb piece of psychological exposure, is tied up with the histrionic business of clearing up a largely artificial mystery. And this makes us question for a moment the central purpose of the novel, when something so profound and real is made, however briefly, to serve the end of something so trivial and confected.

Dickens's fiction always leans towards melodrama, which is neatly characterised by H. W. Fowler, who observes that 'the melodramatist's task is to get his characters labelled good and wicked in his audience's minds, and to provide striking situations that shall provoke and relieve anxieties on behalf of poetic justice'. Dickens is always provoking anxieties so that he can relieve them later; and many of his characters, particularly the bad ones, are very clearly labelled indeed. Consider the repeated images of the moustache and the teeth by which we are taught to recognise the villainy of Blandois (*LD*) and Carker (*D & S*) respectively, and contrast these with the really sinister Orlick (*GE*) who has no obvious badge of evil, but frightens and haunts us because his threatening nature is so clearly seen and rendered without additional moral artifice. Carker has certainly greater presence than Blandois; and it is not that his smile that ne'er came from the lungs is an inappropriate or accidental image of his villainy, only that it is overworked and is used on the strength of its conventional association with evil, rather than as a natural symbol or sign of it.

(viii) SENTIMENTALITY AND MORAL CONVENTIONS

In its dependence on association melodrama is related to sentimentality. Everyone knows that we must be prepared for sentimentality in Dickens; but he is not always sentimental in the same way. A characteristic example of one kind, which has struck all readers, is his use of the word 'little' in connexion with his suffering heroines—Little Nell, Little Em'ly, Little Dorrit; Little Paul as well. There is no reason to suppose that the suffering of small people is any more (or less) painful and poignant than that of big ones. But one can see immediately that a big Em'ly would start off at a marked psychological discount in the reader's tenderer sensibilities. Little things (especially children) are instinctively felt to be defenceless and hence pathetic: so Dickens yanks at our heart-strings by asking us to think of them as if they stayed children (Em'ly's apostrophe takes the process a little further) and to associate a particular kind of pathos with something which is in reality quite distinct from it. So again, because Dickens loves children, everything connected with them, however foolish, has a special aura attached to it. Johnny in *Our Mutual Friend* cannot pronounce 'beautiful', which is in itself a drawback; but because Johnny becomes almost a symbol of redemption from the agonies of living, it is somehow a point of virtue that he can only say 'boofer': by association the qualities of one characteristic (childish innocence) become attached to another (childish incompetence) which does not deserve them.

It is as well to distinguish a sentimentality which eats into the novelist's view of the world and prevents his seeing reality as it is, from one which simply affects his expression, though the second kind may well come to infect his way of feeling and seeing. In *Dombey and Son* (xxiv) there is a contrived scene in which Florence overhears a woman telling her little niece about Florence's sad situation: the woman speaks feelingly of Mr. Dombey's neglect of Florence, and it is natural that Florence should feel deeply the contrast between the stranger who understands and her beloved father who disregards and despises her. She weeps; or rather, as Dickens puts it:

> More of the flowers that Florence held fell scattering on the ground; those that remained were wet, but not with dew.

What is sentimental here is not Florence's tears, which are natural enough, but Dickens's oblique way of describing them, and his insistence on associating the whole scene with conventionally 'poetic' images of innocence in the flowers and the dew, which have in truth nothing to do with the scene at all. The language shies away from direct and open expression, and cheapens the experience by a sly and indirect approach to it. For the expression cannot be wholly detached from the attitude it expresses, and indirect language is a frequent sign that Dickens wants to pull more emotion out of the reader than the situation calls up of itself. So he will not look at Ruth Pinch for what she is—an ordinary, decent, honest, inexperienced girl with whom there is nothing strange in John Westlock's falling in love (*MC,* xlv, etc.); he must play a coy and simpering game with the reader, the silliness of which is not only an insult to our intelligence, but shows how little real interest he takes in Ruth herself.

It is sentimental to attach feeling to something simply on the grounds of external associations, or to graft on to a situation a sentiment to which it does not naturally give rise of itself. Dickens's treatment of certain death scenes is notably sentimental: the death of Little Nell has become something of a locus classicus. In fact it is almost exclusively the death of children or young people which moves him to extravagant or unreal emotionalism. By contrast, the death of Barkis (*DC,* xxx) is eloquent and moving because it is so simply and straightforwardly given and even allows, without detracting from the odd pathos of the scene, for a little wry humour in the invocation of a particular piece of local traditional lore. Now I do not mean to suggest that such occasions are not most especially sad: the death of the young and unfulfilled must always be sad. But what happens in these cases is that Dickens does not let the fact of death speak for itself, revealing its own emotion: he very nearly eliminates the fact, covering over the sadness with a haze of optimistic sentiment which conceals the real emotion which can only be grounded in the real situation. Paul Dombey himself dramatises and distances his own death by the image of a boat on a stream fast approaching the sea. And Dickens uses this to dodge out of looking straightforwardly at his end:

> The golden ripple on the wall came back again, and nothing else stirred in the room. The old, old fashion! The fashion that came in with our first garments, and will last unchanged until our race has run its course, and the wide firmament is rolled up like a scroll. The old, old fashion—Death!
>
> Oh thank GOD, all who see it, for that older fashion yet, of Immortality! And look upon us, angels of young children, with regards not quite estranged, when the swift river bears us to the ocean! D & S xvii

Significantly that is the end of a chapter, and the next one takes us far away. The real agony of the scene is simply not there, nor is it ever realised afterwards. (What can it mean to talk of death as a fashion?) Dickens substitutes an image and a prayer, the piety of which seems quite bogus, because he cannot bear to look at the reality directly.

But much earlier in the novel we have Mrs. Dombey's death, also in Florence's arms, also at the end of a chapter (the first):

> The Doctor gently brushed the scattered ringlets of the child aside from the face and mouth of the mother. Alas, how calm they lay there! how little breath there was to stir them!
>
> Thus, clinging fast to that slight spar within her arms, the mother drifted out upon the dark and unknown sea that rolls round all the world.

This may look superficially much the same kind of thing. Again Dickens uses an image to indicate the fact of the death. But here there is no posturing. And the effect of the image—the dark and unknown sea—is not to push death out of the way, but on the contrary to make it the more present by emphasising just those qualities which make us apprehensive or fearful at its presence or the mere thought of it. There is an awesome finality about this death, which is as far as possible from the wishy-washy optimistics about immortality which make one feel that Dickens is only rather weakly trying to cheer himself up. But Mrs. Dombey is given a little strength to face the unknown: Florence is only a slight spar, a frail little girl, a mere fragment, but her unstinted and selfless love, without any kind of false gesture towards a vaguely hoped-for future, gives courage to face the frightening present. And her involvement in the simple metaphor makes one feel most intimately the attachment on which her mother finally depends.

Sentimentality always involves a miscalling of reality and normally a shrinking from it. It is often the outcome of a shallow or insincere optimism, an attempt to convince oneself or others that things are not really as bad as they seem. So it tends to be cosy (consider the astonishing glimpse of a northern industrial town near the end of *Bleak House* (lxiv), with Esther's rose-embowered cottage as its emblem), and also to shelter behind things as they are. Dickens of course was outraged by very many aspects of the world he lived in: he does not sentimentalise the slums or poverty, even if he underwrites them. But he has little to offer except benevolence in mitigation of such evils. And with him benevolence is sometimes hard to distinguish from a special kind of sentimental self-indulgence. Now as W. E. Houghton has finely shown,

> Benevolence need not . . . degenerate into sentimentality. It does not do so, or only very slightly, in the work of George Eliot. . . . The reason is that for Eliot the essential thing, the foundation of genuine benevolence, is not feeling as such but understanding. It originates in a clear and compassionate perception of human suffering, which then quickens the natural emotions of pity and love; with the result that the emotions are commensurate with what such an object would normally arouse and warrant, and not, as in sentimentalism, too intense for an object which is but dimly perceived. The contrast

may be made in another way that brings out the ethical difference. The sentimental indulgence of pity and love is really self-centred—one enjoys feeling a burst of kindness for those less fortunate than himself—whereas George Eliot's benevolence presupposes a forgetfulness of self in the recognition of our common humanity. (*The Victorian Frame of Mind*, Chap. 11, the whole of which is of great interest for the understanding of Dickens.)

Now Dickens's heroes and more especially heroines are always being dramatically self-forgetful—think of Florence Dombey and Esther Summerson; yet the very insistence on this selflessness shows how insubstantial is Dickens's belief in it: at least for him, this is a prime characteristic which marks them out as *different*; and it is arguably not until Pip so painfully learns what disinterested love really is that Dickens achieves the kind of understanding that Houghton so rightly emphasises in George Eliot.

Secondly, the habit of sentimental categorisation into which, despite what has been said earlier, Dickens so often and so unthinkingly slips (girls are either pure maidens or fallen women, old men are jolly buffoons or grasping misers) gives him a notably conventional attitude to morality. One's complaint is not that he accepted what he found and lived with it: most of us do that most of the time; but that often he did not obey his own novelist's instinct to explore the particular, resting instead in merely conventional notions of right moral attitudes and behaviour. As Humphry House has observed, Dickens was unable to show any struggle towards new moral forms, and this is largely because he felt it so little himself. Consider his treatment of the repentant sinner. All the middle-period novels contain a character, normally a woman, who falls from moral and social grace, but in the end repents. The moral lapse is commonly a sexual one—plainly so in Little Em'ly and Lady Dedlock, less certainly in Edith. All of these come to see the 'error of their ways': indeed it seems as if Em'ly does so as she prepares to commit her 'sin'; but none can be truly accepted back. Lady Dedlock dies (so Sir Leicester's magnanimity is, as it were, for his credit alone, not to make her return to him a real possibility); Edith is shipped off to decent obscurity in France, and Em'ly to Australia—the colonies come in very useful. We should not of course expect, or want, Dickens to follow an advanced 20th-century line on sexual permissiveness, or pretend that he thought such lapses from purity did not matter; and his own relations with Ellen Ternan are not to the point. What is disquieting is that the burden of the sin is so much a *social* one. The point of Em'ly's going to Australia is that she will not be reproached there: there is never the slightest suggestion that Ham might take her to him again, even though she is still all in all to him. Though Sir Leicester is all forgiveness, Lady Dedlock cannot be reunited with him, because she is *known* to be stained: the social obstruction makes the human coming together impossible. After such knowledge, what forgiveness? From Mr. Pecksniff's performances we know very well what forgiveness is *not*; but it seems inescapable that in the Dickens world the fallen woman remains unalterably fallen, and the sinner is never really forgiven on earth, still less rehabilitated. Full payment is always exacted.

Now if Dickens were simply dramatising the ways of society, one could not really make objection to this. It is notable that only in his last novels does the social barrier become assailable: Eugene Wrayburn's marriage with Lizzie Hexam as the culmination of *Our Mutual Friend* is a triumph of the natural, the real human feelings over the artificial rules of society, as the closing chapter ceremonially displays. Lizzie is of course spotless; but to society as represented by the Veneerings and Lady Tippins and Podsnap, her social presumption is heinous. Eugene's refusal to disappear with *her* to the colonies is a sign that now social forms will be tackled at home and not run away from. Still, one cannot imagine Dickens allowing even his reformed hero to marry an Em'ly—to whom he is very far from wishing ill (he does not condemn her to the Furies as he does Quilp or Carker or Compeyson, the vicious and criminal about whom there is nothing more to say and on whom no sympathy need be wasted), but whose sin must be kept alive in her and the reader's consciousness. How serious a matter this is with Dickens can be seen in the solemn warning of evil to come, with its fantastic moral reflexion which David allows himself when he is recounting his games with Em'ly as a child:

> There has been a time since—I do not say it lasted long, but it has been—when I have asked myself the question, would it have been better for little Em'ly to have had the waters close above her head that morning in my sight; and when I have answered Yes, it would have been.
>
> DC iii

This is the voice not of true understanding, but of a man in the grip of a purely social morality; for alas Dickens is not intending this as a distasteful example of David's tendency to self-righteousness. When we reach the moment of Em'ly's elopement itself, the language becomes portentous and self-important again:

> A dread falls on me here. A cloud is lowering on the distant town, towards which I retraced my solitary steps. I fear to approach it. I cannot bear to think. . . .
>
> xxxi

And when finally the truth is out, there is curiously little shock, except indeed to the reader's sensibilities at the blatant faking of the letter that Em'ly is supposed to have written to Mr. Peggotty:

> If even you, that I have wronged so much, that never can forgive me, could only know what I suffer! I am too wicked to write about myself. Oh, take comfort in thinking that I am so bad. . . .
>
> xxxi

How vulgar this is! and in what a painful contrast to the insight Dickens has so recently shown in the picture of Em'ly clinging to Mr. Peggotty just before separating herself from him and her home, as she thinks for ever. The language of the letter is incredible, as it would not have been had she said, as surely such a girl would, 'Try not to think too hardly of me': if she suffers so intolerably, why does she go off? The whole performance has been invented solely to give the force of her own supposed self-condemnation to an action about which Dickens wishes to take a high moral line. I am not asking Dickens to approve Em'ly's flight, only insisting that the rhetorical verbiage of the letter shows that he is more interested in keeping up the moral tone of his novel than in how a young girl in Em'ly's predicament really would behave: she has ceased to be the object of an artist's insight and become instead a preacher's moral example.

Dickens's use of religion or religious imagery seems normally to confirm such tendencies in him. He was a sentimental optimist in religion who invoked God at certain appropriate times, particularly deaths (Jo, Paul, etc.), but without ever conveying much sense of His presence either to character or author: He is there rather to give comfort at times of need, after which He can be conveniently stored in a literary cupboard until the next time. When the Wickfield family is in real danger from Uriah Heep and David asks if there is nothing to be done, Agnes replies, 'There is God to trust in!' (*DC,* xxxix). To be sure there is. But who can believe in a God invoked in so casual a way? For all His ready appearance in their mouths, He means nothing profound, and certainly nothing specific to any of them. For Dickens the Church was, as House says, a national depository of good feeling; but the nature of the feeling or its object was always left vague. Of course Dickens's respectable and also his good people all go regularly to church; but church-going seems little more than a necessary piece of social behaviour. One is much more aware of the activities of false or hypocritical religionists—Stiggins, Heep, Chadband—but the clergymen of whom Dickens approves show their respectability by keeping decently quiet about matters religious, except on formal occasions when the performance is indeed a formality. Mr. Crisparkle in *Edwin Drood* is almost the only instance of a really upright cleric with some spirit.

So Dickens is in many ways a decidedly conventional moralist, whose constriction within the attitudes and forms of his time did considerable harm to his perception and awareness of human particularity. Evildoers are always paid out in the end, and the good normally rewarded. Moreover the rewards are of a notably conventional cast. I have already (p. 90) remarked on Dickens's tendency to let his heroes and heroines enjoy the self-approving glow of virtuous self-denial, only to recompense them later with the very thing they have renounced. This is a particular offence in first-person narratives: in Chapter xxxv of *Bleak House* Esther rejoices that, after her disfigurement, she has not to take on the hard job of writing to Allan Woodcourt to release him from a commitment which he had not by then entered into:

> Oh, it was much better as it was! . . . I could go, please God, my lowly way along the path of duty, and he could go his nobler way upon its broader road.

Now as every reader knows, not only does she get her husband by the end of the book, she also gets back her pretty face. And by the convention of the narrative technique Esther of course knows this when she congratulates herself on something very different half way through. Dickens never lets self-denial be its own reward, and so he never lets it be real self-denial—at least not until *Great Expectations*, and even there he was persuaded to relax his original bleak but humanly truthful ending and requite Pip with Estella's hand. That is one kind of reward held out to those who persist in goodness or those who learn wisdom. The other is the goods of this world, and the really lucky or the really blessed get both marriage and money. However much he deplored the many cruelties and inequalities in the world about him, Dickens was no social revolutionary. The reward he held out to working-class virtue was to be lifted into the middle class: in *Our Mutual Friend* Bradley Headstone and Charley Hexam lift themselves out of their murky background by their own efforts and seem to be regarded as selfish vulgarians for doing so; but Lizzie's true virtue and personal reticence earn her a safe social position. Perhaps it is unfair to invoke this novel, which is concerned to challenge social snobbery and does so very effectively at all social levels from Silas Wegg to the Veneering set. But this seems to confirm that Dickens is of the middle middle, that his ideal world is a classless society with all the marks of the middle class stamped on it.

It was his social and to some extent also political conservatism which prevented Dickens from being the reformer that his often penetrating observation of social abuses seemed to call him out to be. G. M. Young finds in him a 'confusion of mind which reflects the perplexity of his time; equally ready to denounce on the grounds of humanity all who left things alone, and on grounds of liberty all who tried to make them better' (*Portrait of an Age*, 2nd edn., p. 50). So, within his fiction and so far as social action was concerned, the energy generated by Dickens's 'comprehensive spirit of humanity' which the *Edinburgh Review* noted as early as 1838, was largely dissipated because, like his heroes, he has benevolence but no social policy. The world was not going to be reformed by a multiplicity of Jarndyces rescuing Coavinses from destitution—as perhaps Dickens half recognised, for there is an irony, nonetheless real for being sympathetic, in Mr. Snagsby's inevitable half-crowns as a remedy for all ills. Jarndyce's benevolence is more thoughtful than Snagsby's, but really no more systematic. The practical benevolence which the *Edinburgh Review* said Dickens encouraged had to be absorbed or transformed into a positive political movement before the evils which he was so conscious of could begin to be eliminated or assuaged.

But without Dickens many of us today would hardly know what those evils were—or indeed a great deal else of the life of his time. House has demonstrated with some force the extent to which Dickens's reticence has led him constantly to understate the brutality, squalor and filth of the scenes in which large parts of his novels must have taken place. We have already noticed how dust in *Our Mutual Friend* is a concealment for us of what to Dickens's contemporaries would have been plain enough. But his reticence was deliberate sometimes about what not everyone can have then known or wanted to know. It is characteristic of Dickens to generalise his descriptions of social evil—we read generally of filth, drunkenness, debauchery and so on; other writers risked their readership by giving more brutal detail than Dickens did. He seems deliberately to have kept himself back from a comprehensive account of the horrors that the reports of many others prove to have been there—partly no doubt from a wish to accommodate as inclusive an audience as possible (family reading always included children), but quite as much because he must instinctively have recoiled from recording the bestiality and corruption which he found so horrible that he would not entirely admit them to himself: a world in which Oliver Twist and Lizzie Hexam could survive their childhood morally untarnished cannot be irredeemably repellent. Thus the exigencies of his plots and his moral schemata limited the range of his report on the world.

Even so, Bagehot was right to dwell on Dickens's ability to bring us imaginatively into such rich contact with the city which as a writer he made so intensely his own: 'He has . . . the peculiar alertness of observation that is observable in those who live by it. He describes London like a special correspondent for posterity' (essay in the *National Review*, 1858). How much, after all, he has seen that no one else seems to have thought worth recording: he gives to so much life that would otherwise be amorphous and rootless a local habitation and a name. One example of this kind must do—the curious habit that Pleasant Riderhood

> shared with most of the lady inhabitants of the Hole, the peculiarity that her hair was a ragged knot, constantly coming down behind, and that she never could enter upon any undertaking without first twisting it into place.   OMF xxix

The detail has no precise function that one can pin down; yet it is more than mere local colour: the slovenly ritual suggests a certain keeping up of forms even in a life so much composed of the grubby and sordid. And who but Dickens would have spotted the difficulty which an undertaker with any delicacy has in asking after the progress of a mortal illness and yet suggest at the same time a sense of moral self-approval in the man just for being so delicate (*DC*, xxx)?

The genius which comprehends such details and conveys how much a part of life they make is one which for all its faults is constantly moved by the utmost generosity of spirit. Everyone can see that Dickens has a natural inclination and affection for the odd—not the out-of-the-way but the odd: he enjoys crazy houses and people with weird names who live in boats. But this is not for the sake of making an anthology of cranks. If his interest in life seems at times undiscriminating, it is because he has an exceptionally alert sense for all the places in which life appears. Life is life, and is to be enjoyed and fostered in all its forms. That this makes Dickens at times soft-centred is un-deniable. One feels that for him the only crime is meanness—wherever it appears, crabbing and limiting life. Yet he can be equally fascinated by watching even this: he is intrigued by Barkis's nearness with his money, even making us feel that there is a perverse sign of life in its very ingenuity; yet without ever trying to suggest that it is anything other than a form of mean-ness. The true artistry of Dickens seems to me above all to lie in his ability to transmit the extraordinary delight and interest he has in all kinds of human activity, and to make us feel so intensely its inexhaustible resilience and fertility.

3

Four Great Novels

(i) 'DOMBEY AND SON'

Dickens's titles do not always tell one much about the real centre of interest of his novels. *Dombey and Son* is an exception. If we go back to the original full title—*Dealings with the Firm of Dombey and Son, Wholesale, Retail, and for Exportation*—we learn immediately that 'Dombey and Son' is a business association; this full title is in certain respects oblique, but this obliqueness can be seen in retrospect to point to the essential irony at the heart of the book. Dombey and Son *is* a firm; but the crucial human relationships of the book are those *between* Dombey and his son, and negatively between Dombey and his daughter. The great central irony, it may be as well to point out at the start, is that Dombey sees the natural relationship of father to son (and indeed all human relationships) only in terms of Dombey and Son the firm, and in so doing destroys the very son on whom he depended, alike for such affection as he could receive and for the continuance of the great business—the son both of the man and of the firm. Dombey's pride, his enormous and overbearing conceit in his own and the firm's prowess and position, is contradictory and self-defeating: in the end, because it is so fatally vulnerable to flattery, it will bring about his own total humiliation and the destruction of the firm in the name of which he has stifled or struck down all human feelings. 'Girls have nothing to do with Dombey and Son' he announces crushingly when young Paul eagerly associates his sister with a loan, which for the children is a spontaneous piece of generosity, but for Dombey his son's first introduction to business and the power of money (x). And having nothing to do with Dombey and Son, girls have no part in his life.

The power of money is the central point of Mr. Dombey's creed. Money, he tells Paul, 'can do anything'—almost anything, as he has enough good sense to admit immediately afterwards (viii). It can buy him a handsome wife, and the price be displayed in the lavish redecoration with which he loads his house and the lavish jewels and dresses with which he loads her. But it cannot buy her subservience any more than it can buy Paul's health or, ultimately, his life or that of Dombey's first wife, though he employed the most expensive physician. When Dombey chooses Dr. Blimber's school for Paul, Mrs. Pipchin believes it an excellent establishment:

> 'I've heard that it's very strictly conducted, and there is nothing but learning going on from morning to night.'
> 'And it's very expensive.'
> 'And it's very expensive, sir', returned Mrs. Pipchin, catching at the fact, as if in omitting that she had omitted one of its leading merits.   xi

Mrs. Pipchin, who has an extremely sharp nose for whatever is to her advantage and for keeping in well with those who can benefit her, is right: for Dombey the expensiveness *is* a leading merit. It enables him to be seen spending money; Dombey, though his investments are always carefully calculated, is no miser. The chief virtue of money is that it is the mark of his own power which it enables him to demonstrate visibly; his chief—indeed his only—preoccupation is with his own grandeur. His conceit and inflexible sense of his own position come out most strongly when he is faced with the hitherto unexampled obduracy of his second wife:

> 'I am not accustomed to ask, Mrs. Dombey; I direct. . . . It is not the rule of my life to allow myself to be thwarted by anybody—anybody, Carker—or to suffer anybody to be paraded as a stronger motive for obedience in those who owe obedience to me than I am myself.'   xlvii

But this is no more than the bringing to a specific focus of the colossal and outrageous general claim he had made before to the trusted, but false, Carker:

> 'I do not hesitate to say to you that I *will* carry my point. I am not
> to be trifled with. Mrs. Dombey must understand that my will is
> law, and that I cannot allow of one exception to the whole rule of
> my life. . . . The idea of opposition to Me is monstrous and absurd.'
> xlii

Thus does Dombey concentrate his power in the exertion of
the *will*, the asserted mental power that stultifies and blights all
surrounding life. And it is ultimately self-destructive: no man's
will can be law: the cruel restrictions of Dombey's own power
have been shown already by his inability to prevent Paul's
death, and will be shown even more emphatically in the sequel.
But more than this: we are made to feel with great piquancy
that Dombey has been an essential (though of course unwitting)
factor in bringing about Paul's death before he could add anything to the firm or anything but pathos to the life of those about
him. Dombey, in identifying himself with the power of his will,
in reducing all others to subservience to his grand conception of
himself, denies all human relationships that can in any sense of
the word be called natural or life-giving. Edith he marries to
enhance himself:

> he had imagined that the proud character of his second wife would
> have been added to his own—would have merged into it, and
> exalted his greatness.
> xl

His daughter, who has nothing to give him but love and selfless
devotion, he disregards and spurns. And Paul, the being in whom
from the start all his hopes for the future are fixed, he treats
simply as a cipher in the firm, even when the child is only an
hour old:

> 'The house will once again . . . be not only in name but in fact
> Dombey and Son; Dom-bey and Son!'
> i

This subjection of the human being in his child to Dombey's
own pride finds pathetic expression in the eagerness with which
he looks forward to Paul's being no longer a child. 'Really he is
getting on', he exclaims when Paul is six:

> There was something melancholy in the triumphant air with which
> Mr. Dombey said this. It showed how long Paul's childish life had

been to him, and how his hopes were set upon a later stage of his existence.

But the forcing process by which Dombey tries to eliminate Paul's youth (note how Dickens brings in immediately after this passage his hot-house metaphor to describe Dr. Blimber's school —'a great hot-house, in which there was a forcing apparatus incessantly at work', where 'Bring him on!' is the Doctor's favourite injunction—it is this which finishes Paul off)—the process has already done its deadly work, when Dombey brings his principles to bear on the nursing of the child.

If Fanny Dombey had survived her son's birth, she would have nursed him as a matter of course; but to Mr. Dombey she had always been so meek a servant of his greatness that he would not have known how to regard her relation to Paul in any light save that of a provider of necessities which had unfortunately to be transmitted through a woman. (Mr. Chick's suggestion of a tea-pot unfortunately will not do, though Dombey would use one in preference if it would.) So it is when Mrs. Dombey dies and Polly Toodle becomes the child's wet-nurse. Only she is not Mrs. Dombey, and in the interest of eliminating all personal relationships she even loses her own name and becomes Richards while in Dombey's employ. And she must be paid:

> 'Oh, of course', said Mr. Dombey. 'I desire to make it a question of wages, altogether. Now, Richards, if you nurse my bereaved child, I wish you to remember this always. You will receive a liberal stipend in return for the discharge of certain duties, in the performance of which, I wish you to see as little of your family as possible. When those duties cease to be required and rendered, and the stipend ceases to be paid, there is an end of all relation between us. Do you understand me?'
>
> Mrs. Toodle seemed doubtful about it; and as to Toodle himself, he had evidently no doubt whatever, that he was all abroad.
>
> 'You have children of your own', said Mr. Dombey. 'It is not at all in this bargain that you need become attached to my child, or that my child need become attached to you. I don't expect or desire anything of the kind. Quite the reverse. When you go away from here, you will have concluded what is a mere matter of bargain and

sale, hiring and letting; and will stay away. The child will cease to remember you; and you will cease, if you please, to remember the child.'   ii

Here the brutal insensitivity of a life based on money and on class is laid bare. So for the natural relationship between a child and its nurse Dombey susbstitutes the inhumanity of the cash nexus, which is here buttressed by the bulwark of class consciousness. Polly, a hired servant, is naturally a member of the working class: just as no personal element is to enter into her bargain with Dombey and Son, the child is not to be attached to her, for that would compromise the superiority of the Dombeys: the only relationship in which the working class can stand to their social superiors is that of being hired, made part of a bargain. Note too how the will is asserted at the end of the quotation in that most formidable way of commanding, merely by the use of the future tense, which seems at first so innocent: Paul will cease to remember, because it is Dombey's will that he should do so. But even Mr. Dombey's power is not strong enough permanently to overcome natural affection. Spurred on by Susan Nipper, whose affection for Florence is spontaneous and unaffected by any social differences, Polly cannot resist going back to see her family, with whom the natural child Florence instinctively falls to playing in a most unDombey-like way. Polly's crime is that she yields to natural affection—which was no part of the bargain. And in doing so she took Dombey's son 'into haunts and into society which are not to be thought of without a shudder' (vi). So, though she has been the perfect nurse for Paul, she must go:

> 'Ah, Richards!' said Mrs. Chick, with a sigh. 'It would have been much more satisfactory to those who wish to think well of their fellow-creatures, and much more becoming in you, if you had shown some proper feeling, in time, for the little child that is now going to be prematurely deprived of its natural nourishment.'   vi

Her feelings were only those of human warmth and family affection. And so Paul is deprived of his natural nourishment, and ultimately he will die of it.

In Dombey's eyes anyone must be honoured to be allied with him in any way; but the suggestion that he shares a human community with those whose only proper function is to be hired is intolerable. So he tries to reduce all such associations to a mere matter of bargain and sale. But it does not work. There is a brilliant scene in which Dombey meets Mr. Toodle soon after Paul's death: Toodle is the stoker on the train taking Dombey to Leamington. (His connexion with the railways is significant, for, despite an ironic note when they are first introduced in Chapter vi, they certainly represent for Dickens an advancing civilisation —it is a train which in the end destroys the corrupting evil of Carker!) Dombey of course does not recognise Toodle, and when Toodle reminds him who he is, immediately assumes that he is begging:

> 'Your wife wants money, I suppose', said Mr. Dombey, putting his hand in his pocket, and speaking (but that he always did) haughtily.
>
> 'No, thank'ee, sir', returned Toodle, 'I can't say she does. *I* don't.'
>
> Mr. Dombey was stopped short now in his turn, and awkwardly, with his hand in his pocket.
>
> 'No, sir', said Toodle, turning his oilskin cap round and round; 'we're a-doin' pretty well, sir; we haven't no cause to complain in a worldly way, sir. We've had four more since then, sir; but we rubs on.' xx

Dombey's awkwardness stands out from this passage: for one thing his expectations have been proved mistaken (a most extraordinary thing in itself), and worse, he is confounded over a question of money. What else could a workman want from him but money? He wants of course nothing but to express his natural sympathy for Dombey's loss; and as Leavis puts it in his excellent essay (*Dickens the Novelist*), 'Dombey's imputation of the money-motive recoils on himself. The stoker, in the simple decency of his human feeling, registers nothing to resent—sees no insult; it hasn't occurred to him that, in such a situation, there *could* be any intention to snub.' In the reader's eyes Dombey's pride has been totally humiliated by Toodle's simple good nature. But to Dombey the worst blow is that Toodle has, by the common gesture of putting crepe round his hat as a simple memorial—*of Paul*—'set up some claim or other to a share in his dead boy' and 'dared to enter . . . into the trial and disappointment of a proud gentleman's secret heart'. The great affront is the reminder of a common humanity which Dombey cannot escape and of the limits to the power of Dombey's will.

The Toodles may live in haunts that cannot be thought of without a shudder; yet while all Mr. Dombey's wealth cannot keep his son alive, they bring up a large healthy family. Until it serves as a sharp reminder of what he cannot buy, then health is in their favour, for it is a sign that Polly will be a good foster-mother for Paul. The young Toodles are all 'plump and apple-faced'—a word which Dickens later overworks, but which admirably suggests the glow of robust health which surrounds the family and is intimately a part with their affection for one another, their easy-going happiness and their lack of concern for the pride of wealth that means everything to Dombey. To Dombey indeed it is quite an offence that someone so poor as Toodle should have so many children—'Why, it's as much as you can afford to keep them!' (ii). Toodle takes up Dombey's word and uses it in the only way in which (with regard to his children) it means anything to him:

'I couldn't hardly afford but one thing in the world less, sir.'
'What is that?'
'To lose 'em, sir.'

While it is an additional irony that it is only after ten years of marriage that Mrs. Dombey has produced a son and that she did not manage to survive, what really strikes home here is that the thing that matters above all to Toodle is the simple human affection that binds his family together and is superior to all considerations of wealth or lack of it.

The Toodles are not sentimentalised: life is certainly not elegant in Staggs's Gardens, where they live:

a little row of houses, with little squalid patches of ground before them, fenced off with old doors, barrel staves, scraps of tarpaulin, and dead bushes; with bottomless tin kettles and exhausted iron fenders, thrust into the gaps.   vi

Florence joins the children in making a temporary breakwater across, not a neat little pond but, 'a small green pool that had collected in a corner'. It is not altogether an attractive picture, the little house is jumbled and noisy; but the squalor brings little harm to the Toodles because they are jolly and uncomplicated and make the most of what comes to them. It is only when Dombey interferes in the family life by sending the eldest child to the Charitable Grinders' school—an institution for the lower orders which parallels Mrs. Pipchin's establishment for the well-to-do—that they are at all upset: through its hideous uniform the school marks out its victims as cut off from natural life, and the effect of Dombey's charitable action is to send Rob thoroughly to the bad.

It is possible to overemphasise the part played by the Toodles in dramatising the play of contrasted values in *Dombey and Son*; and a bare contrast of them and Dombey would doubtless lay Dickens open to the charge of sentimentalising and crudifying the moral subleties of the human situation. It is noteworthy that, whereas in the novels that immediately precede and follow *Dombey—Martin Chuzzlewit* and *David Copperfield*—Dickens largely relies on simple working people (country people, it is worth noting) to enact the living standards that are contrasted with the dead hand of pride and money, by the time he comes to write *Bleak House* and *Hard Times* he can no longer do so, perhaps because he has seen how far they have been brutalised by poverty and industrial conditions. And in *Dombey* itself, the effectiveness of the Toodles as a reminder of what things humanly matter depends essentially on their being allied with others of a quite different social cast—with Toots, Susan Nipper, Walter and his friends, even Cousin Feenix—and ultimately with Florence herself. Toots has claims to be the greatest comic figure in all Dickens's writing: indeed he is one of the great comic figures of all literature. The comedy is of a kind which one immediately recognises as peculiarly Dickensian, combining a delight in oddity, especially of speech, a preposterous brand of personal vanity and a painful self-consciousness. Yet he never allows self to restrain his courage or hamper his good deeds. And his self-consciousness is partly the effect of his extreme delicacy of human perception. Mr. Toots's appearances are always very funny; his inability to achieve any of his own desires even when openings are made for him is always touching; but he has a moral greatness which expresses itself not only in his devotion to Florence, but in the clarity and honesty with which he sees the reality of moral situations and the kind of action they may call for—a sharpness conditioned by simplicity and narrowness of vision. (This moral clarity he shares with another Dickensian simpleton, Mr. Dick in *David Copperfield:* compare Dostoevsky's *Idiot* and Stevie in Conrad's *Secret Agent*.) It is characteristic of Toots's absurd exterior that when ('in a state of mind bordering on distraction', because of his hopeless love for Florence) he is confronted with the news of Walter's return, a romantic cliché springs at once to his lips:

> 'And at this time!' exclaimed Mr. Toots, with his hand to his forehead again. 'Of all others!—a hated rival!'

But he immediately stops short: 'At least, he ain't a hated rival what should I hate him for?', rushes to look at the man instead of the cliché, and spontaneously recognises Walter's excellence:

> Mr. Toots shot back abruptly into the parlour, and said, wringing Walter by the hand,—
>
> 'How-de-do? I hope you didn't take any cold. I—I shall be very glad if you'll give me the pleasure of your acquaintance. I wish you many happy returns of the day. Upon my word and honour', said Mr. Toots, warming as he became better acquainted with Walter's face and figure, 'I'm very glad to see you!'

Toots is never, for all his intellectual dullness, confused between moral reality and pretence of any kind. Yet he could not serve by himself as an antithesis to Dombey, any more than could the Toodles by themselves.

It is worth looking at a characteristic passage to see something of how the astonishing art of the portrait of Toots is achieved. Soon after Paul's death, Toots plucks up courage to call on Florence, but his immense bashfulness almost immediately overcomes him, and all he can find to do is repeat his opening gambit:

'How d'ye do, Miss Dombey?' said Mr. Toots. 'I'm very well, I thank you; how are you?'

Florence gave him her hand, and said she was very well.

'I'm very well indeed,' said Mr. Toots, taking a chair. 'Very well indeed, I am. I don't remember,' said Mr. Toots, after reflecting a little, 'that I was ever better, thank you.'

'It's very kind of you to come,' said Florence, taking up her work. 'I am very glad to see you.'

Mr. Toots responded with a chuckle. Thinking that might be too lively, he corrected it with a sigh. Thinking that might be too melancholy, he corrected it with a chuckle. Not thoroughly pleasing himself with either mode of reply, he breathed hard.

'You were very kind to my dear brother,' said Florence, obeying her own natural impulse to relieve him by saying so. 'He often talked to me about you.'

'Oh, it's of no consequence,' said Mr. Toots hastily. 'Warm, ain't it?'

'It is beautiful weather', replied Florence.

'It agrees with *me*!' said Mr. Toots. 'I don't think I ever was so well as I find myself at present, I'm obliged to you.'

After stating this curious and unexpected fact, Mr. Toots fell into a deep well of silence.

'You have left Doctor Blimber's, I think?' said Florence, trying to help him out.

'I should hope so,' returned Mr. Toots. And tumbled in again.

He remained at the bottom, apparently drowned, for at least ten minutes. At the expiration of this period, he suddenly floated, and said,—

'Well! Good morning, Miss Dombey.'

'Are you going?' asked Florence, rising.

'I don't know, though. No, not just at present,' said Mr. Toots, sitting down again, most unexpectedly. 'The fact is—I say, Miss Dombey!'

'Don't be afraid to speak to me', said Florence, with a quiet smile, 'I should be very glad if you would talk to me about my brother.'

'Would you, though?' retorted Mr. Toots, with sympathy in every fibre of his otherwise expressionless face. 'Poor Dombey!

I'm sure I never thought that Burgess and Co.—fashionable tailors (but very dear), that we used to talk about—would make this suit of clothes for such a purpose.' Mr. Toots was dressed in mourning.

xviii

The depth of humour in this passage is not fully evident without the context of Toots's other appearances—the grotesque inappropriateness at this point of his own special line, 'It's of no consequence', only being funny and touching together because Toots habitually uses it to get himself out of displays of emotion which embarrass him. Here he is abashed at Florence's remark about his own spontaneous kindness to Paul, something that was very far from being of no consequence, and his only self-defence is to use one of his pitifully small range of conventional phrases. Even this is not quite enough, and he withdraws to the safer ground of his own well-being, his repeated announcement of which is not in the least a matter of self-centredness but rather an expression of his feeling that any other subject is too delicate to be encroached upon. The short paragraph of narrative in the middle of this dialogue is irresistibly funny, but again the humour is touched with Toots's pathos and delicacy: like Mr. Chick with his humming, Toots is happiest when he can chuckle; but instinctively realising the inappropriateness of this on an occasion still of deep sadness for Florence, he only increases his embarrassment. There is no shell whatsoever to Toots: his heart is always exposed. Even the prize expression of his personal vanity, his gorgeous clothes, takes on a pathetic aspect: the rich mourning is still an adornment to Toots's person, but it is also his richest tribute to Paul. Toots has immense difficulty in making human contacts, but his moral insight is impeccable.

None of those characters in the novel who may be said to stand for natural affections, for the heart about which Mrs. Skewton talks so much and so falsely, has much social manner (with the possible exception of Cousin Feenix, whose aimless good will and gentility turn out so impressively firm and genuine in the end). Unlike Mrs. Skewton and the Major and Carker, who calculate their manner to create an impression which has nothing to do with reality, Toots and Susan Nipper and Walter and Captain Cuttle and Florence have no protective covering: their inner nature shows plainly for all to see, and in consequence they suffer when it meets the hard crust of the calculators and pretenders and self-seekers: Susan is dismissed when she speaks her mind to Dombey, Walter's openness is really responsible for his being sent on a voyage that nearly kills him, Captain Cuttle is wounded by Carker and only his imperfect intelligence prevents his seeing how Dombey snubs him. It is a natural characteristic of those whose motives come from the 'heart' rather than the head, who are moved above all by outgoing feeling, that they are so often at the mercy of 'those not unprecedented triumphs of calculation that are always at work on number one', of those too who believe in the primacy of material power and wield it.

Of this group in the novel Toots and Susan Nipper are certainly the most successful creations: in them there is a reality sharply and vividly perceived. In this they go with those other keenly realised figures, Mrs. Pipchin, the Blimbers, Mr. Feeder B.A. and Perch. The pathetic and wavering Miss Tox belongs here too and is in a different creative class from her acquaintances the Chicks—figures of characteristic Dickensian satire whose comic effectiveness depends on the totally predictable nature of their actions. Mrs. Chick is hardly personalised at all; but though the initial description of Miss Tox may at first pass merely as another piece of typical Dickensian extravagance, it is on the contrary closely observed from the real:

> The lady thus specially presented was a long, lean figure, wearing such a faded air that she seemed not to have been made in what linen-drapers call 'fast colours' originally, and to have, by little and little, washed out. But for this she might have been described as the very pink of general propitiation and politeness. From a long habit of listening admiringly to everything that was said in her presence, and looking at the speakers as if she were mentally engaged in taking off impressions of their images upon her soul, never to part with the same but with life, her head had quite settled on one side. Her hands had contracted a spasmodic habit of raising themselves of their own accord as in involuntary admiration. Her eyes were liable to a similar affection. She had the softest voice that ever was heard; and

her nose, stupendously aquiline, had a little knob in the very centre or key-stone of the bridge, whence it tended downwards towards her face, as if in an invincible determination never to turn up at anything.   i

How well one knows that type of tiresome self-effacing person! Yet we know Miss Tox essentially because Dickens shows her to us. For example, in the first sentence of this paragraph, Dickens has not just thought up an amusing image to help in his description: this is how he actually sees Miss Tox, and hence how we see her too. As with all great pictorial artists, Dickens's vision is defined by the terms and modes in which he communicates it: there are not several equally possible alternative ways of giving us Miss Tox's faded gentility, for this is not faded gentility in general, but the particular quality of one individual creature; so only one set of words will exactly do, for only this set defines exactly what the artist has seen. And because Miss Tox is an individual, constantly under observation, her reactions and behaviour in a new situation cannot, like Mrs. Chick's, be precisely foreseen. This is not to say that Mrs. Chick does not do admirably the job she is in the novel for—to represent a particular kind of mindless self-conceit, utterly unobservant of essential change and therefore incapable of it herself—a type for which the satirical mode of portraiture is perfectly adapted, inasmuch as satire always distances the reader and sets up the object in a position designed for critical, rather than sympathetic, disclosure. The reality of Miss Tox is perhaps best seen in contrast with Captain Cuttle, whom for the most part Dickens is content to provide with a very limited set of physical characteristics, and equally limited reactions. Yet his rather boring simplicity (it is almost simplemindedness) is not an object of amusement. Captain Cuttle is indeed a very simple man in whom ingenious or sophisticated thought would be incongruous; the objection to him is not that he is not 'deep', but that Dickens has been content with a bundle of *general* impressions. Unlike Toots's pantaloons (which are the natural, though highly individual, expression of his vanity), the glazed hat is only arbitrarily connected with the man, and no amount of repeated appearances make it belong any more closely. Since Captain Cuttle's small range of language and activity rapidly leads to monotony, it is a miscalculation (a characteristic one) on Dickens's part to allow him to occupy so many pages of the novel.

There is a parallel and more damaging weakness in the presentment of Walter—more damaging because he ought to show himself as what Mr. Toots says he is, 'worthy of the blessing that has fallen on his—on his brow', the perfect husband for the girl who represents for Dickens everything perfect in young womanhood. In truth Walter is altogether too softly drawn, too indistinctly seen, his general characteristic much too quickly taken for granted. Like Toots he is the selfless lover who will not intrude himself on his beloved because he feels her impossibly above him in virtue, but his self-consciousness is of an entirely different kind, which his author takes very solemnly as somehow the *sign* of his worthiness. When Captain Cuttle urges him on, he answers in a thrilled operatic manner that surely deceives no one (except the Captain and Dickens and Walter himself):

> 'Oh! would you have me die in her esteem—in such esteem as hers—and put a veil between myself and her angel's face for ever, by taking advantage of her being here for refuge, so trusting and so unprotected, to endeavour to exalt myself into her lover?' 1

One has to remind oneself that this is not supposed to be funny: it certainly would have been if Toots had said it, as he very well might have. It is curious that the Dickens who can expose so devastatingly the falseness of Major Bagstock or Mrs. Skewton cannot see how utterly divorced from the real this stuff is. Dickens intends in speeches like this to show us just how marvellously noble Walter is. The result is a complete failure, because there is no Walter to be seen: no young man has ever spoken like this outside a story-book, and if he did any sensible girl would tell him sharply to stop putting on an act. True selflessness does not draw insistent attention to itself, nor heartfelt feelings express themselves in theatrical language with its claptrap of veils and angels. As elsewhere with his unswervingly upright heroes, Dickens has satisfied himself with an entirely conventional view of nobility which inevitably appears clothed in clichés. (In fairness it ought to be added that Dickens's original intention was that Walter should have gradually gone to the bad among bad company, 'trailing away, from that love of adventure and boyish light-heartedness, into negligence, idleness, dissipation, dishonesty, and ruin'—an idea which he perhaps did right to abandon, not because of the gloom it would have added to the story, but because it would have introduced a largely irrelevant and hence distracting element into the main progress of the book.)

The merely notional quality of Walter is most serious where it casts doubt on the solidity of Florence. It does not matter very much to the centre of the book that Florence's story is given a happy, indeed a cosily happy, ending; and for most of the book Walter is only a happy or sad memory for her—something for which the lack of substance of the real Walter is no disadvantage. But it would be a different vision of Florence from the one that Dickens is careful we should get, which would end in the collapse of her dreams *because* there was no substance behind her ardent images of goodness. To find that she created her aspirations out of what turned out to be a will-o'-the-wisp would be a subject for irony; and there is no trace of irony in the presentment of Florence. But it is only retrospectively that the shadowy conventionality of Walter makes one doubt Florence. Unlike a good many of Dickens's ill-treated heroines Florence retains obstinately a substance and solidity despite all Toots's and Walter's and Captain Cuttle's attempts to idealise her. From the start she is a child with a child's reactions and a child's logic so disconcertingly disruptive of adult convention: when Polly tells her she is wearing a black frock in remembrance of her mother, she retorts simply 'I can remember Mamma in any frock' (iii). Her terror when caught by Good Mrs. Brown (vi) is unfeigned: how completely Dickens has grasped the child's situation, when Florence stands in the street where Mrs. Brown puts her simply because she has been told to by a person who seems to speak with authority, and so responds with the child's instinctive obedience. Florence's continuing devotion to her father, in the face of neglect and then increasing bitterness and even hatred, may be thought implausible; and it would be foolish to deny that some things are badly overwritten. (There is an unpleasant and morbid section in Chapter xxiv, when Florence considers seriously whether she might not achieve her end of winning Dombey's love by dying.) But Florence fosters her image of her father in the almost complete isolation from him that he has decreed. She knows of course that Dombey is not as other fathers. She is, we are painfully aware, acutely unhappy. Even so she has *some* resources—Susan and Mr. Toots and later and more doubtfully Edith—and when these are taken from her and she is eventually face to face with her father's hatred, the horror of it drives her away and, for a time at least, kills the love she has nurtured in such inauspicious circumstances: she is not proof against *anything* that her father brings against her.

> She did not sink down at his feet; she did not shut out the sight of him with her trembling hands; she did not weep; she did not utter one word of reproach. But she looked at him, and a cry of desolation issued from her heart. For as she looked, she saw him murdering that fond idea to which she had held in spite of him. She saw his cruelty, neglect, and hatred dominant above it, and stamping it down. She saw she had no father upon earth, and ran out, orphaned, from his house. xlvii

The wound comes as much from the destruction of her image of him as from the knowledge that she had a right to expect a reality behind the image. And distance, though it gives her strength to forgive him, does not change the new knowledge she has of what their relations are:

> she forgave him everything; hardly thought that she had need to forgive him, or that she did; but she fled from the idea of him as she had fled from the reality, and he was utterly gone and lost. xlix

The devotion of Susan and Mr. Toots is important in giving strength to the picture of Florence. And it is surely not hard to believe that a child with a naturally loving heart, who has after all had her mother's care and love for six years, would not stop loving simply because she is repulsed. But the reality of Florence is principally important negatively, as a constant reminder and proof of how perverted is Dombey's view of her. Perverted indeed; but the impressiveness with which we are shown the increasing hold that obsession has on Dombey makes us realise that it has a corrupt logic of its own. Because Dombey takes so possessive an attitude to people as well as things, Florence's love for Paul means to Dombey that she is trying to steal him away: love equals possession. That Paul instinctively responds and clings to the people—Florence above all—who give him affection and warmth is a sting which Dombey visits on Florence in proportion to his own inability to call out a similar response in the boy. For unlike Carker or Major Bagstock, he is capable of being wounded—and in more than just his pride. Though that and his obsession with the grandeur of Dombey and Son have so grievously contracted the range in which his heart can breathe, when the first Mrs. Dombey is fatally ill,

> he certainly had a sense within him, that if his wife should sicken and decay, he would be very sorry, and that he would find a something gone from among his plate and furniture, and other household possessions, which was well worth the having, and could not be lost without sincere regret.   i

Mrs. Dombey is little more than a piece of the Dombey display; yet the sense of real sorrow remains, and the picture of the hard man puzzled by something in his own reactions which is beyond his calculation is curiously moving. His son of course means much more, because he is so intimately a part of Dombey and Son, and Dombey loved him 'with all the love he had'. When this object of his love and solicitude is taken from him, it is only too natural to the man whose sentiments have become rigidified by his inhuman conception of his own magnificence that he should react in feelings of frustrated envy towards the one who had stirred his son as he could never do, and whose continued life and health are so bitter a reminder of what he has lost, even if not yet a reproach to him for his part in causing the catastrophe: she was 'his own successful rival in his son's affection' and 'the successful rival of his son, in health and life'.

The steady build-up of his bitterness against Florence is most impressive: it is a bitterness, we feel, deriving in part from the very fact that he has treated her so badly, as a self-justification for the ill-treatment, so that her innocence itself can be turned into evidence for turpitude:

> In his sullen and unwholesome brooding, the unhappy man, with a dull perception of his alienation from all hearts, and a vague yearning for what he had all his life repelled, made a distorted picture of his rights and wrongs and justified himself with it against her.   xl

By this stage she has become associated with Edith, his sworn enemy in the grotesquely simplified world he has made round himself. Edith does not seem to me done with much inward knowledge: she belongs to a side of the book where Dickens as so often falls for the glamour of external melodrama and loses touch with the real. Her selfless attachment to Florence is not in itself convincing: I suspect indeed that it is there essentially to serve the theme of Dombey's relations with Florence. And if we can accept a certain unreality at its base, it does serve this theme wonderfully well. For from this point of view we are looking again at reality not direct, but through Dombey's increasingly distorted vision. Florence, who has thwarted him before, who has been able to call out in Paul something beyond his power to reach, now does the same to Edith—so haughty and overbearing to him, so tender towards Florence. There is a remarkable scene in the chapter (xxxv) called with somewhat too heavy irony 'The Happy Pair'—on the night of Dombey's and Edith's homecoming after their honeymoon. Florence sits silently working while he, as she thinks, sleeps. But he is watching her, and gradually a movement of feeling begins in him towards her: 'she became blended with the child he had loved, and he could hardly separate the two'. Slowly and with difficulty—'they were so strange'—he begins to form the words which will call her to him, 'when they were checked and stifled by a footstep on the stair'. Edith comes in:

> As she sat down by the side of Florence, she stooped and kissed her hand. He hardly knew his wife; she was so changed. It was not merely that her smile was new to him—though that he had never

seen; but her manner, the tone of her voice, the light of her eyes, the interest, and confidence, and winning wish to please, expressed in all —this was not Edith.

'Softly, dear Mamma. Papa is asleep.'

It was Edith now. She looked towards the corner where he was, and he knew that face and manner very well.

So they go away, leaving him once again alone—more alone by the pleasure they take in one another and by the distance he had brought himself nearer Florence. There is doubtless an element of calculation in this scene: one realises that it is because it is in Dickens's overall scheme that Dombey must be made to go through yet deeper and more humbling agonies before he can learn a true humanity that the new movement of feeling must at this point be thwarted. There is certainly truth in the perception that Dombey must be brought to the lowest depths before he can achieve self-knowledge; but an even greater writer would not have needed an outside contrivance to bring the reversal about: there is no such device as Edith's abrupt entry in *King Lear*! Yet when this is said, there is a fine poetic truth in Dickens's trick—for from Dombey's point of view there must seem to be almost an inevitability in Edith's coming in to prevent or spoil his best intentions. In his mind Florence's so innocent pleasure (in a world of Dombeys and Pipchins) in the only one who responds to her becomes itself distorted into something cunning and calculated, and he is left 'outside' again.

From this point there is a relentless build-up in the enmity which is eventually to engulf the whole family in the terrible maelstrom of Chapter xlvii ('The Thunderbolt'), in which all the protagonists are caught on a wheel whose movement it is beyond the power of anyone to stop short of disaster. By this stage all have become victims of this appalling marriage, where the bond is one of mutual scorn and hatred. For Dombey, for all his inhuman arrogance, is at least as much a victim as Edith: in his eyes it could not but be an honour and a pride to any woman to be united to him—how then could he conceive the sufferings he would be the occasion of bringing on her? or how appreciate that her feelings on the marriage did not reciprocate his?

In spite of his hideous behaviour, his deliberate humiliation of her by his rebuking her in front of Carker, his refusal or inability to understand that she can have feelings or motives of her own, Dombey's motives in the marriage are in one aspect more understandable than Edith's. For he thinks—and his motives run no deeper than this—that she will be an adornment to his grandeur, that her pride will be added on to his to make the Dombey façade yet more impressive.

But how about Edith? There is a nearly fatal contradiction in the creation of Edith. We are shown throughout the courtship (or rather we are merely told about) a woman whose capacity for affection and all warm feeling have been corrupted and in the end killed by her odious mother, and by her being treated as a slave 'shown and offered and examined and paraded' for sale: She is now virtually without sensations. Yet for the enormity of Dombey's conduct towards her to be realised to the full, she must retain feelings that can be wounded, even tortured: she must in short be able instinctively to love Florence. Dickens seems at one point to be aware of this problem and gives us a picture of Edith supposedly going through the agonising process of decision. Strikingly enough she is seen at this moment not from within but through the eyes of an outsider; it is in fact Carker's first view of her:

> It was that of a lady, elegantly dressed and very handsome, whose dark, proud eyes were fixed upon the ground, and in whom some passion or struggle was raging. For as she sat looking down, she held a corner of her under lip within her mouth, her bosom heaved, her nostril quivered, her head trembled, indignant tears were on her cheek, and her foot was set upon the moss as though she would have crushed it into nothing. And yet almost the self-same glance that showed him this showed him the self-same lady rising with a scornful air of weariness and lassitude, and turning away with nothing expressed in face or figure but careless beauty and imperious disdain.
>
> xxvii

It is a passage of pathetic, almost comic, ineptness. Dickens does not know what kind of struggle is or could be going on inside an Edith at such a time: he has not been able to think of a plausible motivation of her conduct. For essentially there is *no* inside to her, and so all that Dickens can give are the outside spasms which are supposed to go with passion or struggle, the conventional melodramatics which only too obviously reveal the hollow within—bitten lip, heaving bosom, quivering nostril—it is like an anthology of all the stale tricks by which ham actors reveal 'passion'. There is no real woman or real passion here. Nor, as the story goes on, do we get anything essentially different, only the endlessly repeated proud scorn, indomitable haughtiness, supreme indifference and so on—the very phrases do a kind of dance round her image, occasionally exchanging adjectives but no more. Dickens sees merely the external trappings of anguish and sees them moreover in the form of conventional stage melodramatics. Yet he certainly thought he had provided much more: it is of great moment to him that Edith's 'innocence' should be established in the reader's mind before the end of the book. But innocence and guilt are not words that mean much at the level of generality at which Edith is shown, and the reader's sympathies are more likely to be alienated than softened by the melancholy late scene between her and Florence which is only relieved by the delicately sketched presence of Cousin Feenix (lxi).

As if to emphasise the unreality of Edith, Dickens provides her with a moral double in her natural cousin Alice, whose turbid career and grasping mother are, we are to understand, only a distorted reflexion of Edith's. What Alice was transported for we are never told; but it seems clear that her crime somehow included prostitution. And the moral is that Edith's career and the use made of her by her mother are in essence no different from ones that can be legally punished. Alice likewise has a final reconciliation scene (on her deathbed) which allows the soggy Harriet Carker to preach at her and insist, as Florence does to Edith, that she is 'repentant'—though one might have supposed that this would somewhat reduce the force of the moral of her tale. To complete the preposterous pantomime of this side of the novel, Alice owes her going to the bad to an early encounter with and betrayal by Carker.

Carker therefore belongs to that unfortunate side of Dickens's art that contents itself with the merest conventional notions of what people are like. The too often repeated trademarks of his villainy—the wide smile and the white teeth—associate him with Blandois in *Little Dorrit,* the stage villain identified by conventionally sinister tricks of behaviour. Yet Carker has a greatly more real presence than this summary suggests. There are closely observed details which particularise him and yet deepen our sense of his treacherousness—for example his fastidious care for his own appearance, described in terms which contrive to make cleanliness itself seem false:

> Within hair and whiskers deficient in colour at all times, but feebler than common in the rich sunshine, and more like the coat of a sandy tortoiseshell cat, with long nails, nicely pared and sharpened, with a natural antipathy to any speck of dirt, which made him pause sometimes and watch the falling motes of dust, and rub them off his smooth white hand or glossy linen, Mr. Carker the Manager, sly of manner, sharp of tooth, soft of foot, watchful of eye, oily of tongue, cruel of heart, nice of habit, sat with a dainty steadfastness and patience at his work, as if he were waiting at a mouse's hole.   xlii

The image of the sunbeam washing out the colour from his hair is one which Dickens triumphantly re-uses in *Hard Times* (see p. 135); the nails are not only pared but sharpened (as if they were claws); the glossiness of his linen associates itself with the white skin to suggest a whited sepulchre; the careful ordering of phrases at the end of the sentence makes one realise immediately how his 'niceness of habit' is itself an expression of his cruelty of heart; his 'dainty steadfastness' makes one aware in the curious clash between adjective and noun of something both ruthless and hidden, for steadfastness is characteristically open and even blunt, while to be dainty is to be selective and particular. And his insinuation of himself into Edith's confidence is altogether convincing: it is done simply through the power of knowledge and the skill to use it without scruple to display the weakness of his adversary, a weakness which he reveals only to her on the unspoken condition of her surrender to his methods and proposals. He knows that he can humiliate Edith and make her dependent on him, because he knows the exact nature of her relations with Dombey and can profess to sympathise with her distress:

receive him as one who had the privilege to talk to her of her own by slow and sure degrees [she] had been led on by his craft, and her pride and resentment, to endure his company, and little by little to defiant disregard of her own husband, and her abandonment of high consideration for herself.   xlvi

The real strength and greatness of *Dombey and Son* lie in the theme announced by its title, which includes not only Dombey and his immediate connexions but the subtle and varied web of human relationships by which Dombey's philosophy and way of life are revealed as the distorted, life-killing thing they are. It is a remarkable triumph of art to give direct force to that last phrase: for it is Dombey's philosophy that kills Paul. Yet Dombey is not caricatured as a monster without humanity. Perverted and self-induced though most of them are, Dombey's sufferings are not imaginary; nor are they merely arbitrarily attached to a being otherwise without capacity for feeling. It is the triumphant theme of the book that love is in fact stronger than pride. Dombey's pride has its fatal weakness in its vulnerability to flattery, so that he cannot see the danger of Carker underneath his nose. He has crushed human sentiments under the majesty of his greatness; yet they remain incipiently alive and on occasion force themselves momentarily near the surface of his consciousness. When his greatness finally crashes they are all exposed and raw: there is nothing to shield him from the truths he has trampled on, and the retributive agonies he suffers are real enough to reduce him to the wreck of emotions pathetically stranded among the rejoicings of the happy ending. There is a 'clear evening' ahead for Dombey after the storm of his life, without passion or energy. But (apart from the unfortunate little scene with Captain Cuttle and Sol Gills) his ending is not cosy. Though on a casual reading Dombey's final appearances may seem blatantly designed to touch the reader's tender emotions, the last paragraphs are extremely delicate and moving. Calm though the evening is, it cannot eliminate or even reduce the sense of loss, all the more agonising for its being (as he now knows) self-caused. Despite the large-scale weaknesses that the book undoubtedly contains, *Dombey and Son* is among the most consistently powerful, as it is the most sombre, of Dickens's longer novels.

(ii) 'HARD TIMES'

The history of the reputation of *Hard Times* has been curious and is perhaps revealing about certain habits of mind which can prejudice the full satisfaction to be gained from reading Dickens or any really creative novelist. Soon after its first appearance Ruskin thought it 'in several respects the greatest [Dickens] has written', a book which 'especially should be studied with close and earnest care by persons interested in social questions'. Shaw was equally enthusiastic fifty years later, seeing the novel as a new start for Dickens, the beginning of his great period, when he moved from ridiculing individuals to indicting the nation. Nevertheless it was not a popular favourite, and until quite recently has probably been Dickens's least-read novel. And most Dickensians have evidently felt that it needed some kind of apology or at least explanation.

Hard Times is certainly not a book which it is easy to fit into the conventional account of Dickens: it is exceptionally short—no more than a third of the length of *David Copperfield*; its descriptive passages, whether of place or character, are spare, brisk, to the point, without any of the garrulous diversions which readers familiar with the earlier books would have looked for. It is in fact sparing in the creation of 'character' at all: the persons in the tale have an existence precisely calculated in relation to what they are there to do, and there is nothing left over. Shaw argued that it was the 'mercilessly faithful and penetrating exposures of English social, industrial, and political life' in the books from *Bleak House* onwards which made people prefer the earlier ones; but this does not explain the particular avoidance of *Hard Times*. *Hard Times* is perhaps the most obviously 'social' of all Dickens's novels; and it is worth remark that both Ruskin's praise and Shaw's concentrate on its value as an instrument of social analysis and reform. But Dr. Leavis's essay in *The Great Tradition*, which has been much the strongest influence in working a change of view, approaches the novel as a work of literary art, not as a piece of illustrated sociology or social history; and it has been curious to find lately a reaction to his high critical acclaim taking the form of an attack on the novel for its inadequate social documentation, for Dickens's failure to understand the particular social movements he is supposed to have been satirising. Gradgrind for example has been held to be simply a burlesque parody of the new (or not so new) craze among political economists for statistics. But keen as is Dickens's (very likely not always accurate) sense of the roots of social wrongs, it seems to me narrowing and uncritical to regard this wonderfully well-organised novel as simply a piece of somewhat misdirected political satire.

For all the very characteristic ironic social observation in several brilliant portraits (Bounderby, Harthouse, Mrs. Sparsit), *Hard Times* is a tragedy; and the tragedy centres not, as most people seem to have supposed, on Stephen Blackpool but on Mr. Gradgrind. Moreover it is a work of uniquely intense and concentrated poetry, the moral action of which cannot be understood without an awareness of the working of a delicate and complex poetic language. But whereas the fog in *Bleak House* and the dust-heaps in *Our Mutual Friend,* which everyone hears about, make comparatively inert but largely repeated images, in *Hard Times* images drawn from different situations render vivid and precise our understanding and evaluation of a particular human experience, and then give way to others, so that we have a constantly evolving dramatic language wonderfully sensitive to the developing human drama which it points and reveals. Consider a passage in the book which Dr. Leavis has made justly famous— that in Chapter ii when Mr. Gradgrind, having terrified Sissy into silence, lights on Bitzer to tell her what a horse is:

> The square finger, moving here and there, lighted suddenly on Bitzer, perhaps because he chanced to sit in the same ray of sunlight which, darting in at one of the bare windows of the intensely white-washed room, irradiated Sissy. For the boys and girls sat on the face of the inclined plane in two compact bodies, divided up the centre by a narrow interval; and Sissy, being at the corner of a row on the sunny side, came in for the beginning of a sunbeam, of which

Bitzer, being at the corner of a row on the other side, a few rows in advance, caught the end. But, whereas the girl was so dark-eyed and dark-haired, that she seemed to receive a deeper and more lustrous colour from the sun when it shone upon her, the boy was so light-eyed and light-haired that the self-same rays appeared to draw out of him what little colour he ever possessed. His cold eyes would hardly have been eyes, but for the short ends of lashes which, by bringing them into immediate contrast with something paler than themselves, expressed their form. His short-cropped hair might have been a mere continuation of the sandy freckles on his forehead and face. His skin was so unwholesomely deficient in the natural tinge, that he looked as though, if he were cut, he would bleed white.

At one level this is a description of the schoolroom and the physical appearance of the two children heightened by meta-phorical language. But the metaphor not only gives particular vividness to the visible contrast between the two: the physical differences are realised in such a way as to establish them as symbolic of profound moral and spiritual differences. Sissy's complexion is not simply dark, it is lustrous (a word which conveys her human richness with almost Keatsian directness), and the life-giving sun emphasises and adds to her rich natural resources. Bitzer by contrast is so unwholesomely pale as to appear physically unnatural: not only is the effect of the sun to draw out of him any natural colour, but his very blood, the carrier of life round the body, seems to have lost its true character when the humanity was drained out of him. The final image of the paragraph conveys Bitzer's essential inhumanity with an unforgettable chill vividness. Yet throughout there is no sense of the metaphorical language being strained to express something that is not in the situation, so that Dr. Leavis rightly notes 'the force . . . with which the moral and spiritual differences are rendered here in terms of sensation, so that the symbolic intention emerges out of metaphor and the vivid evocation of the concrete'.

So consummately does Dickens relate plot and character to his central theme in *Hard Times* that one can easily, as one reads, miss the art with which the theme is developed out of the symbolic contrast presented in this paragraph. Sissy is a failure in the school—she is just 'an affectionate, earnest, good young woman and—and we must make that do', as Mr. Gradgrind observes (xiv), with a truthfulness whose significance he is at the time entirely unaware of. Bitzer on the other hand is the ideal pupil whose absorption of the Gradgrind system into himself is so complete that almost all human characteristics are eliminated and he is as it were totally mechanised. Again, Sissy's glowing health is not merely a physical characteristic: it is the expression of her spontaneous life, which comes from an instinctive source deep within her and expresses itself naturally in kindness, gratitude, love, and a refusal to consider human beings as mere elements in a calculus; whereas Bitzer is emptied of all feeling and everything else that cannot be tabulated. He is not activated by malice: as he says in his moment of temporary triumph near the end (xxxvi), he is not planning to take Tom back to Coketown out of animosity. As a true product and exponent of the Gradgrind philosophy he is moved only by self-interest ('I am sure you know that the whole social system is a question of self-interest'), the workings of which are determined by reason alone. It was a characteristic of Sissy, by contrast, that, well before he had other reasons to question the adequacy of his philosophy, Mr. Gradgrind 'had become possessed by an idea that there was something in this girl which could hardly be set forth in a tabular form' (xiv), something 'not an ology at all' as Mrs. Gradgrind pathetically puts it when she is near to death (xxv). Sissy's presence in the house, though it is not to be explained according to the philosophy, is both the sign of ultimate grace in Gradgrind (Bounderby recommends simply that she be turned out as a bad influence) and a large part of the means of bringing him to such capacity as he gains to repair the damage he has caused. And she can do this because in opposition to the philosophy of facts she sees people as individual human beings, not as items in a statistical table.

The demonstration of this truth in Sissy's 'wrong' but human answers to McChoakumchild's statistical questions (ix) is perhaps a little crudely worked in, but she makes an essential point, in answering his challenge about the prosperity of the nation, by saying, 'I thought I couldn't know whether it was a prosperous nation or not, and whether I was in a thriving state or not, unless I knew who had got the money, and whether any of it was mine'. The truth of this only comes home to Gradgrind when he is faced with the wretched Tom and sees at last what it means for a real human being (one of his own children) to be a figure in a table. Gradgrind is utterly shocked that *his* son should have come to this, but the answer, as Tom shows with remorseless Gradgrind logic, is in the figures:

> 'So many people are employed in situations of trust; so many people, out of so many, will be dishonest. I have heard you talk, a hundred times, of its being a law. How can *I* help laws? You have comforted others with such things, father. Comfort yourself!' xxxv

Some critics have argued lately that Dickens's satire on statistics misfires, that he is aiming at the Utilitarians but had so little understanding of what they really stood for that the book parodies Utilitarianism to the point of travesty. Certainly Dickens had the Utilitarians and political economists very much in mind in writing *Hard Times*: he refers to Gradgrind's 'hard, utilitarian face', and aimed to pillory what he saw as the economists' habit of collecting statistics and dealing with human problems in terms of them alone. It is true enough that Dickens was well off the point if he believed that he was capturing the essence of John Stuart Mill's or even Bentham's thought in the teaching methods practised in Gradgrind's school. But Dickens of course knew the school was a caricature: otherwise he would not call the teacher McChoakumchild. And when we consider the education that Gradgrind gives his own children, Dickens's picture is, as Edmund Wilson pointed out, confirmed in remarkable detail in the account given in Mill's *Autobiography* of his own education and his subsequent collapse into illogical despair, in which, Wilson remarks, 'the tragic moral of the system of Gradgrind is pointed with a sensational obviousness which would be regarded as exaggeration in Dickens'. Furthermore the appositeness of the imagery of Dickens's criticism comes home when we recall the 'felicific calculus' which was at the root of Bentham's system of ethics—the view that human obligation can be summarised in the single duty of promoting the greatest happiness of the greatest number, and that quantity of pleasure (which could, ideally at least, be calculated) could alone be considered the criterion of happiness.

However, a more general answer can be made to this criticism, one more relevant to our consideration of *Hard Times* as a novel, and not a mere social documentary. The only facts that Bitzer knows are those that can be tabulated and added up: such facts represent dead things, just as Mr. Gradgrind's statistical clock 'knocked every second on the head as it was born'; for only dead things are unchanging and therefore suitable for permanent tabulation. So calculation comes to stand for a total mechanisation of life in which human and spiritual qualities are eliminated. It is hardly a caricature that in such a system people no longer have names but numbers (Sissy becomes 'Girl number twenty')—for easier computation: when you start numbering workmen as 'hands' and disregarding their individual humanity, it is a short step to thinking of them only as elements in a percentage. The Gradgrind calculus therefore, the philosophy that only numbers count in political economy, is indeed something that Dickens is attacking head on; but he sees it too as the public expression—a natural symbol—of what one may sum up as the bureaucratic view of human life; and against this view the lesson of *Hard Times,* that only individuals matter, is alas by no means a stale one today when the pressures of standardisation (which involves numericalisation) are so great.

Gradgrind's tragedy is the result of his ignoring Sissy's kind of truth for Bitzer's (the two act as choric opposites through the book, though also active in its dramatic development). In his opening encounter with Sissy, Gradgrind tells her that in his school they do not want the kind of knowledge of horses that she can bring—the deep intimate knowledge which comes from working and being with them. Rather they want Bitzer's knowledge, which counts the horse's teeth and tells its age. Gradgrind is nevertheless not another Bounderby: for he is possessed by an *idea*—repellent in itself but disinterestedly held and applied, something truly believed in, and hence very different from the vain and false blustering pride of Bounderby. He had, he says, 'only meant to do right':

> He said it earnestly, and to do him justice he had. In gauging fathomless depths with his little mean excise-rod, and in staggering over the universe with his rusty stiff-legged compasses, he had meant to do great things. Within the limits of his short tether he had tumbled about, annihilating the flowers of existence with greater singleness of purpose than many of the blatant personages whose company he kept.   xxix

It is this uprightness and singleness which make him capable of tragedy, and the mean and demoralising smallness of his vision which make it inevitable. His system has all but blinded him to the reality of human emotions; yet he keeps a crucial sanity through his love for his children (and especially Louisa)—so strangely and grimly expressed, but an essential part of him nevertheless. And it is through the disasters that he has led them into that he is brought face to face with the truth about his own system: it is his tragedy that he is brought to humility and a kind of wisdom through a catastrophe, to those he has (in his way) genuinely loved, for which he was ultimately responsible. The tragedy is the more painful in that the deepest permanent harm is done not to himself but to those who—it is his saving grace— ultimately mean more to him than he himself does. Loasui and Tom are sacrificed to Gradgrind's obsession, their lives ruined irreparably: Dickens does not flinch here.

The quality of this tragedy is brought most directly to the surface in the scene in which Gradgrind tells Louisa of Bounderby's proposal of marriage, and in those of her return home and of Tom's final exposure. The proposal scene (xv) repays the most careful reading and re-reading, for its delicacy of perception and rendering need great flexibility and sensitivity in the reader. The scene is too long to be considered in detail here; but fortunately there is Dr. Leavis's brilliant analysis, which should be read by all interested in understanding the depth of Dickens's art. What I wish to stress is the profound seriousness and penetration that Dickens achieves through his wonderfully precise control of tone. The situation is in itself ironic, and Dickens's treatment is ironic likewise, though it is essential that we understand that the word in this context in no way suggests anything detached or supercilious. The irony derives from, indeed expresses, a deep and sustained sympathetic understanding of a melancholy human situation—of two people most intimately related, and at a crucial juncture for one of them, whose speech is almost totally at cross-purposes. Mr. Gradgrind is disconcerted and embarrassed by the calm with which Louisa receives the news (astonished after all that his system *should* have evidently had such a triumph in her); so he counters her forthright use of the simple terms of human feeling with statistical irrelevancies which for him express feeling as well as everything else. But when she tries to bring home to him the human reality of the life he has prepared for her and to inject human meaning into the relationship he holds open to her, his misunderstanding is total:

'Louisa, I have not considered it essential to ask you one question, because the possibility implied in it appeared to me to be too remote. But, perhaps I ought to do so. You have never entertained in secret any other proposal?'

'Father,' she returned, almost scornfully, 'what other proposal can have been made to *me*? Whom have I seen? Where have I been? What are my heart's experiences?'

'My dear Louisa,' returned Gradgrind, reassured and satisfied, 'you correct me justly. I merely wished to discharge my duty.'

'What do *I* know, father,' said Louisa in her quiet manner, 'of tastes and fancies; of aspirations and affections; of all that part of my nature in which such light things might have been nourished? What escape have I had from problems that could be demonstrated, and realities that could be grasped?' As she said it, she unconsciously closed her hand, as if upon a solid object, and slowly opened it as though she were releasing dust or ash.

'My dear,' assented her eminently practical parent, 'quite true, quite true.' xv

It is easy to misread this passage if one is not alert to the variations of tone within it. Mr. Gradgrind is blinded by all his preconceptions to the true meaning of what Louisa says, so that her 'almost scornful' reminder of all that she has missed from her young life only served to confirm him in his idea that her up-bringing has been ideal. When Louisa speaks again, the scornful tone continues, and there is something near sarcasm in her use of the word 'light' to characterise the natural affections she is starved of: her speech stands out like a challenge to her father, who cannot see beyond his idea that it presents a desirable truth. And the gesture of her hand, a commonplace of passion, gains real poignancy from the reminder of mortality ('life is very short') which Dickens's image hints at. It points back perhaps to a narrative paragraph which occupies one of the long pauses dur-ing the dialogue and gives a mournfully haunting sense of the unimaginable loss from which each suffers:

> From the beginning, she had sat looking at him fixedly. As he now leaned back in his chair, and bent his deep-set eyes upon her in his turn, perhaps he might have seen one wavering moment in her, when she was impelled to throw herself upon his breast, and give him the pent-up confidences of her heart. But, to see it, he must have overleaped at a bound the artificial barriers he had for many years been erecting, between himself and all those subtle essences of humanity which will elude the utmost cunning of algebra until the last trumpet ever to be sounded shall blow even algebra to wreck. The barriers were too many and too high for such a leap. With his unbending utilitarian, matter-of-fact face, he hardened her again; and the moment shot away into the plumbless depths of the past, to mingle with all the lost opportunities that are drowned there.

First the slow, methodical and laborious construction of the wall which keeps so much of humanity from Mr. Gradgrind; then the reminder of a power far greater than any that Gradgrind can wield and of the standards against which his will be found want-ing; finally the image which conveys so movingly how irrevoc-able is the loss which this moment has marked, carried off into the irredeemable pastness of time: the image is throughout figur-ative, but observe how 'drowned' picks up the earlier 'plumbless depths' to give a physical heaviness accentuating the sensation of something lost beyond recall.

Something of the same combination of pathos and irony comes in the last, climactic scene in which Gradgrind is brought face to face with the disgraced Tom and finally witnesses the collapse and worthlessness of the system:

> They all three went in; and Mr. Gradgrind sat down, forlorn, on the clown's performing chair in the middle of the ring. On one side of the back benches, remote in the subdued light and the strangeness of the place, sat the villainous whelp, sulky to the last, whom he had the misery to call his son.
>
> In a preposterous coat, like a beadle's, with cuffs and flaps exaggerated to an unspeakable extent; in an immense waistcoat, knee-breeches, buckled shoes, and a mad cocked hat; with nothing fitting him, and everything of coarse material, moth-eaten, and full of holes; with seams in his black face, where fear and heat had started through the greasy composition daubed all over it; anything so grimly, detestably, ridiculously shameful as the whelp in his comic livery, Mr. Gradgrind never could by any other means have believed in, weighable and measurable fact though it was. And one of his model children had come to this! . . .
>
> 'If a thunder bolt had fallen on me,' said the father, 'it would have shocked me less than this.'
>
> 'I don't see why,' grumbled the son. 'So many people are employed in situations of trust; so many people, out of so many, will be dishonest. I have heard you talk, a hundred times, of its being a law. How can *I* help laws? You have comforted others with such things, father. Comfort yourself!'
>
> The father buried his face in his hands, and the son stood in his disgraceful grotesqueness, biting straw; his hands, with the black partly worn away inside, looking like the hands of a monkey. The evening was fast closing in; and, from time to time, he turned the whites of his eyes restlessly and impatiently towards his father. They were the only parts of his face that showed any life or expression, the pigment upon it was so thick.   xxxv

It is one of the highwater marks of Dickens's art, a passage which contains the satirical *reductio ad absurdum* of the Gradgrind philosophy, whose total effect is yet very far from satire, though the situation has its elements of comedy—the oddity of Gradgrind sitting on a clown's chair, Tom's grotesque costume, his bizarre self-excusing logic which is so close a parody of Gradgrind's own that his father has no answer to it. But yet again the overall impression is not comic. The brilliantly observed detail acts to create and define the confused emotions of the scene. The clown's chair in the middle of the ring intensifies our sense of Gradgrind's forlorn loneliness amid the ruins of all his life's beliefs; Tom's fantastic and squalid appearance gives physical expression to his disgrace and suggests, as he bites straw and has hands like a monkey's, that he has become something less than human. Yet the intensely-felt human emotion starts out from that last reference to the terrified movement of the eyes, at a moment inescapably of the most profound silence. The scene is an extremely painful one—of painfully expressed emotion; yet nowhere is there any attempt to underscore the emotion: it is created simply through Dickens's scrupulous fidelity to fact, arising with complete naturalness from the presented situation.

Ruskin thought Bounderby overdrawn, and there is possibly a miscalculation in making him 'as near being Mr. Gradgrind's bosom friend, as a man perfectly devoid of sentiment can approach that spiritual relationship towards another man perfectly devoid of sentiment' (iv). Yet this is the mark of how far Gradgrind has tortured his own humanity; and there is nothing inconceivable in the mindless extreme of Bounderby's 'rugged individualism': England is full of Bounderbys. He is of course, at the root of his bullying, a fraud: in the world of facts in which he pretends to live, his vaunted image of the self-made man is based on a mean and corrupt fancy—a piece of grim but peculiarly apt irony, for he represents the extreme of insensitivity to the claims of humanity, a grossly coarsened expression of the self-centredness which is a fundamental principle of Gradgrindery and finds different forms in Bitzer, Tom and Mrs. Sparsit, all offshoots of the system which deliberately excludes the outgoing human emotions of love and gratitude (all that Sissy stands for) as sentimental, and incalculable, fancies. Bounderby has a crucial role in the development of the plot; and he is also vital as the dominant expression of the domineering ungenerosity of spirit which has made Coketown what it is—a

town as hideous and corrupting in its larger human relations as
it is in its murderous physical depression of the individual human
spirit. But Bounderby also acts as a kind of objectification of the
logical conclusion of the Gradgrind system, the abstract given
concrete expression: this is what it comes to in the end, just as
the wreck of Tom's and Louisa's lives are by-products of its des-
tructive passage through the world.

At the other end Sleary's circus has a similarly representative
function in the novel, though it too is active in the plot. Like
Sissy, who is one of them, the people of the circus stand at the
extreme of uncalculating, spontaneous human affection; though
innocent of anything that would pass for learning with Gradgrind,

> yet there was a remarkable gentleness and childishness about these
> people, a special inaptitude for any kind of sharp practice, and an un-
> tiring readiness to help and pity one another.   vi

Clearly there is a danger of sentimentality in such a conception;
yet there is astonishing sureness and tact in Dickens's presentation
of the company. Superficially they are not very attractive: there
is a brusque insolence and assumption of superiority about
Childers and especially Kidderminster (albeit a suitable reaction
to Bounderby's bullying roughness); and Sleary himself is described in terms which seem to promise the worst:

> a stout man . . . with one fixed eye and one loose eye, a voice (if it
> can be called so) like the efforts of a broken old pair of bellows, a
> flabby surface, and a muddled head which was never sober and
> never drunk.   vi

The circus is not glamourised; but nor is Dickens misled by superficial appearances, nor allows us to be. The qualities of Sleary
that matter are not his asthmatic, boozy ugliness, but his un-
wavering uprightness and gratitude. There is a certain sentimentality and sloppiness as well as coarseness in him, but it is a
sentimentality in the created character, not in the creation.
Dickens sees him vividly as a person, with his roundabout approach to any subject and his suddenly and briskly coming to

the point. And there is an irresistible rightness in his coming to deliver the formal moral. For not only is he alone in a position to do so, with a certain odd kind of social status as well as a real moral authority; but he has also the kind of simple direct speech, once he gets to his subject, in which alone the statement will be natural and telling.

> 'It theemth to prethent two thingth to a perthon, don't it, thquire?' said Sleary, musing as he looked down into the depths of his brandy-and-water; 'one, that there ith a love in the world, not all thelf-intereth after all, but thomething very different; t'other, that it hath a way of ith own of calculating or not calculating, whith thomehow or another ith at leatht ath hard to give a name to, ath the wayth of the dogth ith!'   xxxvi

This inescapably *is* the moral of the story—the moral truth that underlies all the action and evaluates it. It is dramatised throughout in the complex interaction of plot and character. But the novel loses nothing in dignity and gains much in directness by containing this simple statement of it at the end. Sleary is perfectly in character to speak as he does; and it is with the most delicate reminder of the human limitations of his speaker that Dickens tempers the solemnity of the moral formulation: so much of Sleary is, one might say, of the flabby brandy-and-water kind, that the clarity of his vision of moral truth is all the more notable for the reminder of his particular weakness in the middle of the speech: even if his immediate inspiration does come from the depths of his brandy-and-water, its permanent truth is something apart from this.

This episode is one of many in the book where one can see at a glance how intensely dramatised is the whole narrative method. The book is singularly free from authorial intervention; it also depends little on interior monologue or static description. Everything comes out of the action; and the physical action, as in a stage drama, contains in itself and makes plain all the moral developments and the significance of plot and situation.

Hard Times is a brilliantly plotted novel: the action moves on with a sense of single-minded, concentrated energy which is nearly unique in Dickens and brings him for a moment perhaps close to Conrad. In all his other novels (save *Great Expectations*) one has the impression from time to time of passages—sometimes whole chapters—which are merely preparatory to a great static set-piece. *Hard Times* too has its great dramatic scenes, but they are, to adapt Mrs. Sparsit's metaphor, more in the nature of temporary landings on a continuous staircase, along which the action moves inexorably to its inevitable culmination: the action in fact moves on through them. In *Hard Times* alone in Dickens's work this sense of inevitability grips the whole story. Gradgrind's tragedy grows out of the evil that he has allowed to dominate him before the start of the book; and from the opening chapters, where the tension between two opposing attitudes which will in the end wreck all his schemes is laid bare, the ultimate catastrophe is—though we do not of course know at this stage what form it will take—inescapable. The psychological development of Louisa and Tom, who will carry the main weight of the consequences of evil, is completely sound in inception and admirably convincing in narration. Louisa's emotional life has no outlet except her affection for her brother; the only way she knows to turn her adult life to any account is to use it for him. So she marries Bounderby under pressure from Tom, and in the emotional desert of her marriage not surprisingly finds herself attracted by the one person—Harthouse—who, for whatever selfish intent, at least looks on her as someone who has an existence of her own. Likewise Tom has been brought up in the school that teaches that we are so constituted as to respond only to appeals to self-interest, and so he becomes 'that not unprecedented triumph of calculation which is usually at work on number one'. The grim humour of this brilliant sally at the expense of Gradgrindery is not only perfectly judged but seems so spontaneously felicitous that it is something of a surprise to find it a reworking of a joke that Dickens has used, much less effectively, at least once before (see *Nicholas Nickleby*, lx—'the only number in all arithmetic that I know of . . . is number one'). Tom, emotionally raw and ignorant of all self-knowledge, inevitably sinks into debt, and from there, utterly uneducated as he is in any sense of human responsibility, the descent into small-scale bank robbery is a small and natural step.

Here one may notice the exceptionally skilful and economical interweaving of different strands of the plot. Tom's mean and cunning trick on Stephen Blackpool is entirely convincing in itself: he does not really *mean* any harm to Stephen and cannot of course be expected to foresee the terrible outcome; but simply seizes on the chance to pass suspicion away from himself, the truth being that he does not see Stephen (or anyone else) as a person who can suffer but only as an object that his self-interest can make use of, as he has made use of Louisa. At the same time the subsidiary theme of the isolation and alienation of Stephen is carried further by Tom's act, as it is by the previous move when Bounderby sacks him; this likewise serves a double purpose while at the same time increasing our understanding of what Bounderby represents: here he is above all the unintelligent bullying fool, seeing himself as gaining favour with the workmen by getting rid of the man they have turned against.

Nevertheless in the side of the book that concerns itself directly with the industrial scene there is a serious flaw, both in Dickens's perception and in the plot that derives from it. That Dickens should have only a very imperfect knowledge of factory life in northern England need cause no surprise, and some mis-calculations could be expected. What is less excusable (though still eminently characteristic) is his confident use of quite in-adequate material to establish a point of view which he had come to hold through ignorance or prejudice. He made a visit to Preston to watch a strike but got little from it, and did not in fact include a strike in his novel. And as Shaw remarked, the scene of the trade union meeting addressed by Slackbridge, ill-organised and ill-conducted, is simply the expression of middle-class ignor-ance: Disraeli and Mrs. Gaskell, disadvantaged though they might seem to be by birth or sex, knew these workers better. Dickens simply deplores the trade unions without qualification and therefore gives us a union agitator in Slackbridge who is dis-honest and sinister: possibly there were Slackbridges in the early trade union movement (though Shaw thought him inconceivable), but even so he would be inadmissible in this role in this book, which (as Dr. Leavis says) aims so much at the representative. For Slackbridge is the chief presented evidence against the trade union as such: the union is an evil thing, and the proof is in the crookedness of the leader, who is accordingly shown to be a scoundrel, and the workers at best fools for joining a union, misled by a confidence man. Just so, any opponent of the union for whatever reason (Dickens dodges this issue) qualifies to be a martyred hero of nearly ideal goodness, instead of a characteristic example of an honest workman. Stephen's fellow-workers' action in sending him to Coventry is thus made to appear almost luridly unfair.

Why does Dickens spoil his case by this special pleading? Does he need a specially good man to suffer from his wretched wife and to make Tom's crime all the worse? Surely not. If Stephen had been simply unfortunate (as so many were), even perhaps a bit surly and inclined to keep to himself, though a good worker, he would have served Dickens's other purposes equally well—indeed better, for we should not have mistrusted the reasons presented for his actions; and the reason for his not joining the union could have arisen naturally. The weakness as it comes out in the novel is not alone that Stephen is thus sentimentalised in language and reactions, and that Dickens has shown his ignorance of a very important social and economic movement, but that by bringing out the trade union theme in this particular way he sets up a cross-current that he cannot control and which is imperfectly related to the book's central theme. Gradgrind's story, though a personal and particular one, has nevertheless the representative generality of true tragedy, seen compassionately yet with a disinterested care for truth. It is arguable that in Stephen's case Dickens did not care enough about the real-life situation to go to the trouble of finding out what the truth was. And so we are incomparably more moved by Gradgrind's wretchedness than by Stephen's, whose story all the time seems to be twisting our arm.

(iii) 'LITTLE DORRIT'

Little Dorrit opens in a prison in Marseilles. The particular prison plays no part in the novel after the first chapter, and the two men we see locked up together in it, though they are necessary later on to the working out of the machinery of the plot, are a good way off the main centres of interest. So there is something apparently casual about this introduction. The scene itself is vividly evoked—both the permanent, damp chill of the noisome prison and the contrasting heat and glare outside, where

> everything that lived or grew was oppressed by the glare—except the lizard, passing swiftly over rough stone walls, and the cicala, chirping his hot, dry chirp, like a rattle. The very dust was scorched brown, and something quivered in the atmosphere as if the air itself were panting.   I, i

But no scene in a novel should exist for its own sake alone, and the place of this one is for long unexplained.

Only a vague, heavy ominousness possesses us, hinting at things we should perhaps rather forget, like the hush on the sea 'so deep . . . that it scarcely whispered of the time when it shall give up its dead'.

In Chapter ii we are still in Marseilles, but only by coincidence —with an entirely fresh group of characters, travellers from the East impatiently waiting to be released from another, more temporary, kind of prison in which they have been quarantined. By Chapter iii we have left Marseilles—for ever as it turns out— and are with one of the travellers just arrived in London on a Sunday evening. It is no release for him or the reader: Arthur Clennam sees around him a million people imprisoned by their labour among the 'sweet sameness' of 'miles of close wells and pits of houses, where the inhabitants gasped for air'—people whose only secular want on a Sunday could be 'nothing but a stringent policeman'. The sound of a church bell recalls for Clennam the horrible Sundays of his Calvinist boyhood when

> like a military deserter, he was marched to chapel by a picket of teachers three times a day, morally handcuffed to another boy;

when his mother sat all day behind a Bible

> bound, like her own construction of it, in the hardest, barest, and

straitest boards, with one dinted ornament on the cover like the drag of a chain, and a wrathful sprinkling of red upon the edges of the leaves—as if it, of all books! were a fortification against sweetness of temper, natural affection, and gentle intercourse.

The ominousness we felt in the first chapter now seems to be settling towards a specific focus in the savagely heartless travesty of Christianity in which, we soon discover, Mrs. Clennam still lives. But the chain of prisons has by no means been exhausted and for the present there is only a tenuous and again apparently casual connexion between Mrs. Clennam's self-inflicted prison and the one we meet next—the Marshalsea, which is once again a literal prison and becomes the central and dominating image of the book.

If we have read much of Dickens already we shall be sure by this stage that the various threads started and dropped in seemingly so careless a fashion in these early chapters will all later be picked up and tied together with more or less ingenuity. But the very casualness, the haphazard collocations, of the opening are in fact significant of Dickens's overriding preoccupation in *Little Dorrit*: almost everyone in the book is in a prison of some kind, self-made or forced upon him, no one can escape entirely the taint of prison life—the constraint which symbolises, as we shall see, our refusal or inability to face the truth about ourselves, so that we remain bound in an illusion of which the prison is an expression, sometimes depressing and sometimes eerily comforting. 'Humankind cannot bear very much reality,' and the prison is an escape from responsibility as much as a restriction on freedom.

So it is with Mr. Dorrit, in whose sufferings and their consequences the main psychological exploration is concentrated. He is imprisoned for a debt incurred in circumstances which he is too simple-minded to understand, doubts whether it is worth unpacking his bag (he is to stay so short a time), and lives to become the oldest inhabitant and the Father of the Marshalsea. But like the brandy-soaked prison doctor he finds peace there:

Crushed at first by his imprisonment, he had soon found a dull relief in it. He was under lock and key, but the lock and key that

kept him in kept numbers of his troubles out. If he had been a man
with strength of purpose to face those troubles and fight them, he
might have broken the net that held him, or broken his heart; but
being what he was, he languidly slipped into this smooth descent,
and never more took one step upward.   I, vi

He soon comes to belong more to the prison than to anywhere
else: the circumstances of his long incarceration can even become
a source of pride, so that 'a disposition began to be perceived in
him to exaggerate the number of years he had been there'. It is
one of the shrewdest of Dickens's penetrations to see that this
limp, vain, self-centred man can survive, can even come to
relish, an imprisonment, which goes near to killing the far more
purposeful, unself-seeking Clennam, thwarted by his inability
to do anything to redeem himself or his situation. In this Mr.
Dorrit may seem to resemble Cavalletto who so gamely makes
the best of his situation in the Marseilles prison. But Cavalletto
is, as it were, only there by accident and in passing: Mr. Dorrit,
alternating between vain and ludicrous boasting and a despairing
self-pity, is 'in either fit a captive with the jail-rot on him'
(I, xix) with 'the impurity of his prison worn into the grain of
his soul'. It is a characteristic manifestation of Dickens's technical
mastery in the presentation of Mr. Dorrit that the stark, even
brutal truth about him should be made so bluntly clear amid the
pathos of his situation: so we are held back from squandering
the wrong kind of pity on him and at the same time given a
sharp reminder of the permanent warping of a man's soul which
is involved—for it is easy, after a while, to live the prison life, so
much so that the free air becomes lethal to those who have habi-
tuated themselves to the fetid, unnatural atmosphere within its
walls.

  Mr. Dorrit is eventually released: the scene in which he learns
that he will soon be free to leave the Marshalsea—a situation rich
in danger for any novelist with a tendency to indulge in exces-
sive sentiment or whose comedy frequently turns to the sardonic
—is in fact one of the most adroit and affecting in the book.
Clennam and Little Dorrit have come to break the news as
gently and carefully as they can. Nevertheless:

Her agitation was exceedingly great, and the tears rolled down her
face. He put his hand suddenly to his heart, and looked at Clennam.

I, xxxv

The sudden movement of Mr. Dorrit's hand to his heart, where
it stays through the following dialogue, suggests apprehension,
almost fear, a physical constriction reflecting alarm as much as
fantastic and previously unimagined hope. In the end Clennam
must tell him by means of a question:

'Tell me, Mr. Dorrit, what surprise would be the most unlooked for
and the most acceptable to you? Do not be afraid to imagine it, or to
say what it would be.'

He looked steadfastly at Clennam, and, so looking at him,
seemed to change into a very old haggard man. The sun was bright
upon the wall beyond the window, and on the spikes at the top. He
slowly stretched out the hand that had been upon his heart, and
pointed at the wall.

'It is down,' said Clennam. 'Gone!'   I, xxxv

'He seemed to change into a very old haggard man.' It is as if
Mr. Dorrit, so long protected from the disintegrating touch of
freedom, begins to crumble when the first real air is let into his
room, like those bodies which are artificially preserved by being
sealed in a dry, airless chamber and which turn to dust as soon as
the tomb is opened. The spikes on the wall which, when Mr.
Dorrit's imprisonment had been most oppressive to both him
and his daughter, 'made a sullen purple pattern on the sun', now
gleam at the moment of release not only from prison but of the
tensions by which Mr. Dorrit's little life was kept together.

The seeming recovery that follows is given with astonishing
delicacy, precision and economy. 'He remained in the same attitude looking steadfastly at' Clennam. The shock literally leaves
him speechless—and what might so easily be a cliché, a merely
conventionally imagined reaction, impresses us here as being
utterly natural and right. Clennam and Little Dorrit talk in consequence into a void, as if soliloquising, while Mr. Dorrit's only
reactions come in the physical changes of his body:

He yielded himself to her kisses and caresses, but did not return
them, except that he put an arm about her. Neither did he say one

word. His steadfast look was now divided between her and Clennam and he began to shake as if he were very cold.

After he has been given wine he at last leans back in his chair and weeps. But it is only when Clennam tells something of the discovery of the fortune that is to release him that Mr. Dorrit's voice comes back as he begins to reassert the family pride in his new-found ability to patronise by means of his wealth. From stillness he turns to sudden movement, when he hears of Pancks's service:

'He shall be—ha—he shall be handsomely recompensed, sir,' said the Father, starting up and moving hurriedly about the room.

The movement seems uncontrolled, aimless, for the new freedom leaves the long-caged animal with no knowledge of how to use it. There is something ominous again in the sudden voluble speech as in the sudden movement, as Mr. Dorrit comes to realise the pride of his new riches.

'Everybody,' he said, 'shall be remembered. I will not go away from here in anybody's debt. All the people who have been—ha—well-behaved towards myself and my family shall be rewarded. . . . I particularly wish, and intend, to act munificently, Mr. Clennam.'

There is a moment of sardonic comedy when Clennam offers to lend him money for the time being.

'Thank you, sir, thank you. I accept with readiness at the present moment what I could not an hour ago have conscientiously taken. I am obliged to you for the temporary accommodation. Exceedingly temporary, but well-timed—well-timed.'

An hour ago Mr. Dorrit would have accepted as a gift anything that anyone chose to offer; yet he had been superior towards Clennam whose 'obtuseness on the great Testimonial question was not calculated to awaken admiration in the parental breast' (I, xxii), and whose delicate generosity towards the family had expressed itself lately in less obvious ways than in the giving of tips. At the end of the little speech Mr. Dorrit becomes quite grand:

> 'Be so kind, sir, as to add the amount to these former advances to which I have already referred, being careful, if you please, not to omit advances made to my son. A mere verbal statement of the gross amount is all I shall—ha—all I shall require.'

He can now patronise Clennam as well as the inferior 'Collegians', and it is for him a gesture of something like abandon when, with so much newly at his command, he can ask for 'a mere verbal statement'. Finally with a pathetic pride in his appearance which he is conscious does not accord with his wealth ('I confess I could have desired . . . to have bought a—hum—a watch and chain' . . . but 'button my coat across the chest, my love. It looks—ha—it looks broader, buttoned') he shows himself to his fellow-prisoners, receives their homage 'with great urbanity and protection', and as he withdraws, says of them ' "Poor creatures!" in a tone of much pity for their miserable condition'—miserable at least as much because they will now lose their 'protector' as because they cannot, like him, leave the prison.

The scene moves from pathos to comedy, but it does so with consummate tact, and the steadiness of observation remains absolute throughout: the comedy, fairly gentle though it is at this point, is not in the least cosy. On the contrary it reveals as much of Mr. Dorrit's hollowness as the elaborate artifice of his earlier patronising of his 'inferiors' and the grimmer fantasies that come later: it is the comedy, which, as Santayana sees so clearly, reveals 'the moments of our lives . . . in their grotesque initiative and . . . pillories them before our eyes'. It is something which could only possibly be done by an artist intensely aware of *facts* and never, when his vision is clear, allowing ideas or notions to take their place: only through the most acute consciousness of how people actually behave can Dickens make such a scene so tellingly and uncomfortably true to our innermost selves.

The spiritual decay of Mr. Dorrit after his release follows a pattern almost exactly parallel to that of his moral degeneration (the word is Dickens's) before. There are indeed a number of significant echoes and references back to his earlier state, the most striking of which is the scene when, on Mr. Dorrit's return to London from Italy, Young John Chivery comes to pay his respects with a bundle of the cigars which were always so well received while Mr. Dorrit was still a prisoner (II, xviii). Instinctively Mr. Dorrit takes the visit as a taunting reminder of the past which he has been so careful to hide from his rich new acquaintance and turns on Young John savagely: in such a situation his present position is at risk and his pride of place threatened. Yet so clear is Young John's honesty of purpose—he too has his pride and is 'too proud to have come' if he had thought Mr. Dorrit would take it ill—that Mr. Dorrit is ashamed. (Such touches of consciousness of common humanity in Mr. Dorrit are expertly placed to keep him from alienating himself from us totally and for good.) The effort of facing reality again—of accepting that he *had* spent so many years in the Marshalsea—makes him tired and ill, and the scene marks a large step in Mr. Dorrit's increasing failure to keep appearance and reality so far apart that his old self will not be recognised in his new surroundings. It is a measure of the complete integrity of Dickens's vision of Mr. Dorrit and again of the steadiness of his perception that for all his shame at his outburst, there is no softening of the edge that divides Mr. Dorrit's dreams from his memories, no chumminess between the 'free' and rich man of the present and the reminder of the bankrupt prisoner of the past, only an armed truce: 'nothing could change his [Young John's] face now from its white, shocked look', and, after he has assured the old man that he is 'too proud and honourable' to speak to anyone else in the hotel about what once was, 'Mr. Dorrit was not too proud and honourable to listen at the door, that he might ascertain for himself whether John really went straight out.'

The scene reveals directly how thin and vulnerable is the protective covering by which Mr. Dorrit seeks to deny, if possible to obliterate, the past. But it also recalls a scene when his likewise newly-won position of 'Father of the Marshalsea' seems threatened—by a testimonial from the wretchedly poor Plornish, who can only afford 'a little pile of halfpence', which Mr. Dorrit interprets as an insult:

> The Father of the Marshalsea had never been offered tribute in copper yet. His children often had, and with his perfect acquiescence it had gone into the common purse, to buy meat that he had eaten, and drink that he had drunk; but fustian splashed with white lime bestowing halfpence on him, front to front, was new.
>
> 'How dare you!' he said to the man, and feebly burst into tears.
>
> The plasterer turned him towards the wall, that his face might not be seen; and the action was so delicate, and the man was so penetrated with repentance, and asked pardon so honestly, that he could make him no less acknowledgment than, 'I know you meant it kindly. Say no more.' I, vi

The moral victory is as clearly Plornish's here as it is Young John's in the later encounter: both men's actions are the natural gestures of spontaneous and generous good nature (Plornish's is more—it shows a moral delicacy which is quite beyond anything Mr. Dorrit could aspire to), and both make Mr. Dorrit ashamed; but both threaten a position which is too frailly held, based, if not quite on fraud, at least on a false view of the world in which he lives. Both in and out of the Marshalsea, Mr. Dorrit leans his life on a false conception of gentility. For the Father of the Marshalsea it is a polite fiction:

> With the same hand that had pocketed a collegian's half-crown half an hour ago, he would wipe away the tears that streamed over his cheeks if any reference were made to his daughter's earning their bread. So, over and above her other daily cares, the Child of the Marshalsea had always upon her the care of preserving the genteel fiction that they were all idle beggars together. I, vii

For the 'free' Mr. Dorrit, the wealthy expatriate, vanity and the pretensions of family dignity make him the victim of a sham much the more sinister for being unacknowledged as well as having far greater consequences.

The main human symbol of this new stage in Mr. Dorrit's decline is Mrs. General, whose snobbery and grotesque ideas of propriety make her a relation of Mrs. Sparsit in *Hard Times,* with the difference that she worships money rather than rank.

When the Gowans are discovered to be on Mrs. Merdle's visiting list they instantaneously become acceptable:

> 'A more undeniable guarantee could not be given,' said Mrs. General to Mr. Dorrit, raising her gloves and bowing her head, as if she were doing homage to some visible graven image.   II, v

Mrs. General is a figure of high comedy with her 'papa, potatoes poultry, prunes and prism'; but one can hardly laugh when she announces that 'perfect breeding forms no opinions, and is never demonstrative', for Mr. Dorrit immediately surrenders to her preposterous conception of gentility and the highest human values by allowing her devotion to money to take possession of him also. But Mrs. General is above all sinister in that she gradually takes precedence in Mr. Dorrit's esteem and even affection over Amy herself, whose once paramount position in his world has already been largely sapped by those who can be hired: she would have liked to accompany her father at least part of his way back to England:

> But though the Courier had gone on with the Bride, the Valet was next in the line; and the succession would not have come to her, as long as any one could be got for money.   I, xv

While Mr. Dorrit acknowledged, even in a back-handed way, his dependence on his daughter, a modicum of essential sanity remained to him; now she is replaced by Mrs. General and the hired servants, the real and the symbolic (money-devoted) aspects of Mrs. General combine; and she is only defeated by Mr. Dorrit's providential death.

The parade of gentility which Mr. Dorrit keeps up at the Marshalsea only partially conceals things which are a good deal nastier than the foolish pretence itself. When Little Dorrit innocently looks after and takes by the arm Old Nandy, whom her father has patronised as his 'pensioner' (Nandy is the one person to whom Mr. Dorrit can actually give small amounts of money in much the manner in which he receives rather larger sums from the collegians), it is the summit of humiliation to Mr. Dorrit— for Nandy is a pauper. Unlike Mr. Dorrit, he admits that he has no money; and he has in his honesty gone to the workhouse in order not to impose on his son-in-law—a gesture of more genuine honour and dignity than the spurious forms of gentility which the bankrupt Mr. Dorrit keeps up by sponging on those as poorly off as himself. But family pride insists that the pretence be kept up; and a degradation of real human values is the inevitable outcome.

The root of the corruption of honour in Mr. Dorrit is revealed in progressive detail in a scene (Chapter xix) about half way through Book I. Here he starts by reproving his brother for the slovenly life he leads, pointing to himself as an example of regularity but revealing at the same time how entirely he is a parasite on the good will of others. (There is a notable double edge to his remark that Frederick might be like him if he chose.) When he is left alone with his daughter, the self-centredness changes its point of application and becomes a blatant appeal for sympathy, showing, for all the pathos of the situation, how much he aligns himself with it and sees himself as its only victim. The whine changes to a feeble proclamation of his own dignity in the Marshalsea—'the chief person in the place' (who is nevertheless dependent on all the others), at which he is so moved that 'he burst into tears of maudlin pity for himself, and at length suffering her to embrace him, and take charge of him, let his grey head rest against her cheek, and bewail his wretchedness'; yet two pages later he can solemnly reassert himself to her:

'I am in the twenty-third year of my life here,' he said, with a catch in his breath that was not so much a sob as an irrepressible sound of self-approval, the momentary outburst of a noble consciousness. 'It is all I could do for my children—I have done it. Amy, my love, you are by far the best loved of the three; I have had you principally in my mind—whatever I have done for your sake, my dear child, I have done freely and without murmuring.'

Only the Wisdom that holds the clue to all hearts and all mysteries can surely know to what extent a man, especially a man brought down as this man had been, can impose upon himself. Enough, for the present place, that he lay down with wet eyelashes, serene, in a manner majestic, after bestowing his life of degradation as a sort of portion to the devoted child upon whom its miseries had fallen so heavily, and whose love alone had saved him to be even what he was.

How magnificently sure Dickens's touch is here—the man is so thoroughly known, and the tone of Dickens's own words so triumphantly right: 'an irrepressible sound of self-approval, the momentary outburst of a noble consciousness'—see how the hollow grandiosity is conveyed in the very rhythm of the words. And the concluding authorial comment, so just in its evaluation, so clear-sighted in its exposure of complacent weakness, so free from false sympathy yet so deep in its awareness of how much the life is to blame—how truly we see the extent to which the degraded life has become Little Dorrit's 'portion', her dowry, as well as her allotted fate—the comment seems (as such things do not always in Dickens) to arise so naturally out of the preceding scene that we are hardly conscious of the author intruding at all. It is a masterpiece of tact.

Much later, in Italy, there is a scene between father and daughter in which his very words to her here are reinvoked. Mr. Dorrit, though incapable of true delicacy himself, is a great connoisseur of it in others—where, that is, it affects him. He accuses the long-suffering Amy of indelicacy in constantly reminding him of the life he once endured—not in words, he admits, but by the simple fact that she alone does not gladly enter into the superficial society life and manner which his new riches have bought. So he upbraids her for failing to follow his way—'*I* can eradicate the marks of what I have endured, and can emerge before the world a—ha—gentleman unspoiled, unspotted'—and justifies himself with the same degree of self-approval as when he spoke such familiar words in the prison, though now with a feeling of thwarted anger:

'I was there all those years. I was—ha—universally acknowledged as the head of the place. I—hum—caused you to be respected there, Amy. I—ha hum—I gave my family a position there. I deserve a return. I claim a return. I say, sweep it off the face of the earth, and begin afresh.'   II, v

But of course he cannot sweep it off the face of the earth: the longer he survives his change of fortune, the more morbidly sensitive he becomes of anything that he believes is a hint at what he once was. That there is never any foundation for this morbid suspiciousness makes no difference: the innkeeper who has been browbeaten by Mrs. Merdle into letting her have for a few minutes a room reserved by Mr. Dorrit, the footman who, even more innocently, stands waiting for orders—anything or nothing can become a sign for Mr. Dorrit that he is being mocked and reminded that he was not always what he now is, that there is a 'spot' on his gentility.

The psychology of Mr. Dorrit's decline is rendered in part naturalistically, in part symbolically, but the symbols are themselves so natural that in no way do they obtrude themselves. Prison has sharpened Mr. Dorrit's querulous self-centredness to the point almost of madness, where any hint of the prison which comes from outside produces reactions literally beyond all reason. Hence the treatment of Young John in the interview discussed above. By this stage his mind has become as much a prisoner of its own terror of the prison as his body once was of the prison itself. The Marshalsea has caught up with him again. As he nears his end the marks of physical decay begin to show: he alternates between an intense tiredness, when, in the middle of conversations, he falls momentarily into a profound sleep, and fitful outbursts of undirected energy. He is cross with the world and above all with himself, and on waking takes it out of his brother by bullying him and transferring to him his own illness. What is happening here is a separating of events from their true locations, appearance and reality are no longer joined, and parts of the mind are dissociating themselves from others: the process reaches a climax in the great scene where Mr. Dorrit at a dinner party of Mrs. Merdle's believes himself back in the Marshalsea and makes a speech welcoming the dinner guests into its walls. There is now complete dissociation of time as well as place; and the last few pages of Mr. Dorrit's life are a moving evocation of the final collapse of a mind which has become the captive of a prison essentially of its own making.

This is not to say that Dickens does not present the Marshalsea as a real physical prison, whose restriction for so long of the prisoner's physical movements is one of the main causes of his later mental decay. Imprisonment for debt was in any case a real evil that clearly Dickens intended to speak out against (though the Marshalsea itself had long been demolished by 1855); and the picture of the helpless Mr. Dorrit at the beginning of the book, unable to understand how he has incurred the debt for which he is imprisoned, is of a man at least as much sinned against as sinning, though Dickens does not spare his fecklessness. In the early stages of writing *Little Dorrit* Dickens was going to call it *Nobody's Fault,* a title reflecting primarily the political aspects of the novel, which bulked larger in early plans than in the completed work. It would have given a misleading over-emphasis to one side of the prison theme: Mr. Dorrit always thinks that the fault lies with someone else, but the essential point to see is the extent to which the enforced narrowness of his life combines with qualities inherent in Mr. Dorrit (and at least potential in us all) to produce the creature of self-absorbed and self-engrossing vanity whose only ultimate career is to destroy itself. It is almost inevitable that Mr. Dorrit in moving out of one prison should move into another. His movements have been constricted so long that his mind has lost all power of movement on its own. But in relating such a process Dickens seems to have more in mind than the instinctive self-imprisonment of Mr. Dorrit. After they have spent some time in Italy, it appeared to Little Dorrit

> that this same society in which they lived greatly resembled a superior sort of Marshalsea. Numbers of people seemed to come abroad, pretty much as people had come into prison—through debt, through idleness, relationship, curiosity, and general unfitness for getting on at home. They were brought into these foreign towns in the custody of couriers and local followers, just as the debtors had been brought into prison. . . . They were usually going away again to-morrow or next week, and rarely knew their own minds . . .
> —in all this again very like the prison debtors.   II, vii

The effect here is somewhat forced: the reflexion does not strike the reader as one which would come naturally to Little Dorrit, who is not given to making symbolic comparisons, and the particular comparisons made here have the air of being made more for the sake of the neatness of the parallel than because they impress themselves as natural or inevitable. But undoubtedly society does have its prisoners, of whom Mr. Merdle is the chief. Mr. Merdle turns out to be a fraud, but he is also a victim. His legendary wealth is a burden to him, for it only buys him a place in the society which is Mrs. Merdle's whole reason for existence, but which is no more than an unmeaning abstraction, clothing itself in various frightening forms, such as great dinners and the chief butler, who, after Mrs. Merdle,

> was the next magnificent institution of the day. He was the stateliest man in company. He did nothing, but he looked on as few other men could have done. He was Mr. Merdle's last gift to Society. Mr. Merdle didn't want him, and was put out of countenance when the great creature looked at him; but inappeasable Society would have him—and had got him.
> I, xxi

The chief butler recurs as a symbol of Mr. Merdle's victimisation: he becomes Mr. Merdle's chief gaoler; and with a beautifully unobtrusive touch Dickens shows us Mr. Dorrit as especially suspicious of him when he dines with Mr. Merdle, even fancying the chief butler to have had some connexion with his Marshalsea life.

Mr. Dorrit never learns the truth about himself: his vanity has long ago erected a barrier which his intelligence is far too weak to penetrate. Mr. Merdle half-knows the truth, and thereby deceives himself as much as others. But Mrs. Clennam is a different case altogether. All three reveal the chasm between appearance and reality in human society. In Mr. Dorrit the surface of 'gentility' puts a curtain over the reality of poverty in the present or past; Mr. Merdle is apparently of an impregnable probity but brings ruin on half London; Mrs. Clennam conceals behind the wall of her righteousness a cruelty the reality of which she never comes to terms with. But of the three she is the only one whose prison is entirely self-made: yet even she inherited materials for it in the hideous religion in which she had been brought up and in which she lives, identifying it with her own fierce and narrow will. Her religion, her moral attitude, her self-induced paralysis, the room which has long been the limit of her world, are all aspects of the prison which she has created. But the religion is impious—

> Forgive us our debts as we forgive our debtors was a prayer too poor in spirit for her. Smite thou my debtors, Lord, wither them, crush them; do thou as I would do, and thou shalt have my worship: this was the impious tower of stone she built up to scale Heaven.   I, v

And unlike the other prisoners she exults in her prison, as she bargains with God, certain of a reward for her present suffering and certain in the righteousness of her rigour. She 'reversed the order of Creation, and breathed her own breath into a clay image of her Creator' (II, xxx), and made her savage religion the name for her devilish pride and the excuse for vindictiveness and cruelty. So she proclaims the justice by which she has made others to suffer as she herself suffers, referring both to the savage idol she worships:

> 'If I did not know that we are, every one, the subject (most justly the subject) of a wrath that must be satisfied, and against which mere actions are nothing, I might repine at the difference between me, imprisoned here, and the people who pass that gateway yonder. But I take it as a grace and favour to be elected to make the satisfaction I am making here, and to work out what I have worked out here. My affliction might otherwise have had no meaning to me. Hence I would forget, and I do forget, nothing. Hence I am contented, and say that it is better with me than with millions.' I, xxx

Yet even Mrs. Clennam's life has been one of struggle—'with the whsiper that, by whatever name she called her vindictive pride and rage, nothing through all eternity could change their nature'. When she is finally faced, in Blandois, by a devil stronger than herself, with the knowledge that her secret is no longer hers to keep, her prison cracks, she flees with strength she has not known for a decade to ask forgiveness of the person among those still alive whom she has most injured: it is the only direct sign of her accepting that there are truths beyond and more sacred than those of her religion. Yet even now she cannot free herself from the fetters of the past and continues to insist on her own righteousness:

> 'If this house were blazing from the roof to the ground. . . . I would stay in it to justify myself against my righteous motives being classed with those of stabbers and thieves.'   II, xxx

For the house no longer holds her: she has escaped from it as (partially) from her old religion; and as the prison has lost her it destroys itself and the devil with it. But, like Mr. Dorrit, Mrs. Clennam has been held by it too long to escape entirely, and the shock brings back the prison of paralysis complete and forever.

The two chapters which end with the collapse of the house make a melodramatic climax to the main theme of the novel as splendid in their different way as the previous climax before Mr. Dorrit's death. And they are handled with characteristic ingenuity and skill. Nevertheless the very way in which these chapters sweep one along calls in question the central purpose of a novel which can be brought to a climax with such a device. The bursting asunder of the house has a natural and symbolic grandeur that no one would want to change. But it is only the culmination of the bursting asunder of the mysteries by which the whole elaborate apparatus of the plot has been kept going. Dickens has no master in keeping up suspense by such means, even though the delays in revealing the truth and the artifice by which these delays are kept up may sometimes be tedious; but it is not the highest or most interesting way of sustaining the reader's interest over a long story. Once the mystery is out it holds us no longer (who ever reads a detective story twice?), whereas the story of the slow collapse of Mr. Dorrit is of the profoundest human interest for its own sake, and so it repays repeated re-reading. Episodic though it is, we are held by Mr. Dorrit's story because it sets up, however distantly, certain vibrations in our own: it is intensely a part of the sad music of humanity. To have linked him with the Merdle family is a triumph not only of ingenuity (on Dickens's part, of course), but of shrewdness of perception and judgment: the elaborate but empty and corrupt structure by and in which they live is exactly the trap that Mr. Dorrit's career has prepared him to fall into. What is surely much less happy is the link of the Dorrits with the Clennams (and through them with the Casbys, Meagles and so on) by the forced and intrinsically uninteresting devices of mystery and coincidence, and by the singularly colourless figures of Arthur Clennam and Little Dorrit herself. The two main strands of the novel are made to hang together only by the relationship of Arthur Clennam and Little Dorrit and the mysterious and implausible coincidence of the previous connexion between Mrs. Clennam and Frederick Dorrit. There are of course novels of great worth which are, as it were, like two large areas of land held together only by a narrow isthmus (*Anna Karenina* is the most notable of all); but if such a scheme is to be a success the isthmus itself must be of strong and real interest to the reader. It is a fault of *Little Dorrit* even more than of *Bleak House* that Dickens fails to provide this interest at the point where his two main stories come together. Esther Summerson has probably annoyed more readers than Arthur Clennam has; but at least in her case Dickens faces his problem pretty squarely by making her the principal narrator, so that for all her silly self-depreciation and sentimentality, we are aware of how intimately she belongs to both worlds. A certain amount of the action of *Little Dorrit* is seen through Arthur Clennam's eyes; but his principal moral function appears to be to comment directly on the otherwise unrecognised virtue of Little Dorrit or indirectly (by his honesty in taking the suffering on himself) on the hypocrisy and self-interest of most of the others. Because Dickens has frequently made him a vehicle for his own most sensitive and indeed touchy observations, there is the danger always that he becomes something of a prig: he seems to nag at us as well as at the moral blemishes of other characters. When Little Dorrit visits him late at night he suddenly realises what her wretched physical condition is like:

'And I have no fire,' said Clennam. 'And you are—' He was going

> to say so lightly clad, but stopped himself in what would have been a reference to her poverty, saying instead, 'And it is so cold.'   I, xiv

The scruple is one of the utmost delicacy, and alone the little scene could be very striking: it is in the context of many others in which Clennam plays a similar part of expressing the conscience of the book too openly that the tone becomes unctuous. When the Dorrit family leave the Marshalsea, Little Dorrit gets forgotten—a nice point of irony even if the pathos seems a little obvious. It is Clennam who finds her after she has fainted, and his bringing her down in his arms is the occasion for a fine satirical thrust in Fanny's complaint of Amy's once again being a disgrace to the family, which bursts out as the one explicit notice they take of her. But Clennam must rub in the pathos even further:

> 'She has been forgotten,' he said, in a tone of pity not free from reproach. . . . 'Take care of this poor cold hand, Miss Dorrit. Don't let it fall.'   I, xxxvi

Surely the episode would work on the reader with all the more poignancy if Dickens had not felt the need for Clennam's mechanical conscience to formalise it for us like this.

It is only towards the end of the novel that Clennam comes to be a figure in his own right, separated from his author's consciousness. Then, when he in his turn suffers in the Marshalsea and reacts in a way so different from Mr. Dorrit's, Dickens's study of him becomes impressive and authoritative:

> A burning restlessness set in, an agonised impatience of the prison, and a conviction that he was going to break his heart and die there, which caused him indescribable suffering. His dread and hatred of the place became so intense that he felt it a labour to draw his breath in it. The sensation of being stifled sometimes so over-powered him that he would stand at the window holding his throat and gasping. At the same time a longing for other air, and a yearning to be beyond the blind blank wall, made him feel he must go mad with the ardour of the desire.   II, xxix

By this stage Dickens has no longer any need to use him to establish the moral standards by which the action of the book is judged; and suddenly the portrait is objective and penetrating:

it is in fact the very scrupulousness of Clennam's conscience which nearly kills him when he cannot assuage its torment. He too becomes (though in so different a way) self-absorbed and so in danger of being self-destructive. It is then only the selflessness of Little Dorrit that saves him.

It was at a fairly late stage in the conception and even some way into the writing of the novel that Dickens changed its title and simultaneously started referring to his heroine as 'Little Dorrit' rather than simply as 'Dorrit'. The addition of the adjective inclines the reader to see her (as surely Dickens did too to some extent) in company with Little Nell and Little Em'ly, the misused innocents who are the occasion for so much sentimental special pleading. Little Dorrit is certainly stronger than the others; but the reader's patience is tried by Dickens's repeated insistence on her innocence, and it is significant that on the one occasion on which she shows a certain very justified resentment, Dickens reproves her for it. She asks Arthur to confirm that Mr. Dorrit will pay all his debts on leaving prison and when he does so:

> There was something of uncertainty and remonstrance in her look—something that was not all satisfaction. . . . 'It seems to me hard', said Little Dorrit, 'that he should have lost so many years and suffered so much, and at last pay all the debts as well. It seems to me hard that he should pay in life and money both . . .' . . . The prison, which could spoil so many things, had tainted Little Dorrit's mind no more than this. Engendered as the confusion was in compassion for the poor prisoner, her father, it was the first speck Clennam had ever seen, and it was the last speck Clennam ever saw, of the prison atmosphere upon her.   I, xxxv

It is a curious moment, for it is one of the reader's strongest impressions up to this point, as plainly it is Dickens's and now Little Dorrit's, that Mr. Dorrit has morally paid his debt many times over by his incarceration.

Since, however, the charge of sentimentalism is one that is pretty likely to occur to the reader before he has seen a great deal of Little Dorrit, it is well to be on our guard against its malign converse and to see her in the perspective of her place in the whole novel, a perspective the choice of which is shown by the change in title to be deliberate. Without Little Dorrit the comparative serenity of the end when, against a background of 'the noisy, and the eager, and the arrogant, and the forward, and the vain [who] fretted, and chafed, and made their usual uproar', Clennam and Little Dorrit 'went quietly down into the roaring streets, inseparable and blessed' (II, xxxiv)—without this, *Little Dorrit* would be a pessimistic novel. True, the main sources of evil have been destroyed or neutralised; but the emphasis is so much on the cost in terms of suffering, that any sense of ease at the end must be muted indeed. Doyce may have at last made his own way, but the Circumlocution Office, that central symbol of obstructiveness, of organisations that destroy life, remains. And the whole of the society against which the story of the Dorrits and the Clennams is highlit, of the commercial world in which it is the whole duty of man to keep someone at it or to be kept at it oneself, is one marked by a contempt for or indifference to distinctions between good and evil, seen at its extreme in Blandois and in its most characteristically opportunist form of modish cynicism in Henry Gowan, whom Doyce in a memorable phrase describes as having 'sauntered into the Arts at a leisurely Pall Mall pace . . . I doubt if they care to be taken quite so coolly.' Gowan does not really 'take' art at all: he regards it like everything else as the occasion of a great deal of pious fraud which only the unillusioned and 'disappointed' like himself can see through. He has no real frankness, only a shallow travesty of candour whose main characteristic is its contempt for fineness of feeling:

'I don't like to dispel your generous visions, and I would give any money (if I had any) to live in such a rose-coloured mist. But what I do in my trade, I do to sell. What all we fellows do, we do to sell. If we didn't want to sell it for the most we shouldn't do it. Being work, it has to be done; but it's easily enough done. All the rest is hocus-pocus.'   I, xxxiv

This cynicism allies itself not only with the corruption of values in Blandois and Mrs. General and the bitter vindictiveness of

Miss Wade, but with the whole construction of a society in which it is common for people to 'get rid of a good deal of other people's money, and bear it very well' and in which the selfish and wanton gambling of one man can ruin so many who have never been close to him at all.

What, in the world of *Little Dorrit,* is Dickens to set against that? Principally the small deeds of those whose world is tiny and whose behaviour even comic, but who live by honour even though they may not recognise it by name. Young John is one of these: he is far more honourable than Mr. Dorrit in that memorable interview; and his expression of his uprightness, though touched with a pathos which tips over into comedy, has its own true dignity. When Little Dorrit has rejected his suit, for the offering of which he made himself so pathetically respondent, she knows that she can rely on his never pressing it again. Then:

> as she held out her hand to him . . . the heart that was under the waistcoat of sprigs—mere slop-work, if the truth must be known—swelled to the size of the heart of a gentleman, and the poor common little fellow, having no room to hold it, burst into tears. I, xviii

It is both a touching and a dangerous moment at which sentiment could so easily spill over into sentimentality; indeed one wonders how much irony there is in that contrast between the 'common little fellow' and the 'gentleman'; but Dickens distances himself from the scene just sufficiently by hinting at a certain ludicrousness in the contrast between tawdry finery and a solemn heart, and clinches the effect of comedy by sending Young John back to the Marshalsea composing a new member of the series of epitaphs, which form his staple of daydreams.

Perhaps even more moving is the portrait of Frederick Dorrit whose sad and feeble life, redeemed by complete uprightness (when wealth comes to him he is not at all corrupted—only made more articulate), is shown us in a picture of exquisite delicacy.

> [He] shuffled in again, sat down in his chair, and began warming his hands at the fire. Not that it was cold, or that he had any waking idea whether it was or not.

> 'What did you think of my brother, sir?' he asked, when he by-
> and-by discovered what he was doing, left off, reached over to the
> chimney-piece, and took his clarionet case down . . . . Arthur won-
> dered what he could possibly want with the clarionet case. He did
> not want it at all. He discovered, in due time, that it was not the
> little paper of snuff (which was also on the chimney-piece), put it
> back again, took down the snuff instead, and solaced himself with a
> pinch. He was as feeble, spare, and slow in his pinches as in every-
> thing else; but a certain little trickling of enjoyment of them played
> in the poor worn nerves about the corners of his eyes and mouth.
>
> I, ix

It is another admirable instance of how Dickens keeps his eye
on the real: there is nothing in the remotest bit factitious about
the observation, nor does the sympathetic detail in which the old
man's aimlessness is portrayed show any sign of yielding to an
outpouring of sentiment which the situation does not truly give
rise to. Only, there is that 'little trickling of enjoyment' which is
the sign of a security, indeed a sanity, which is beyond anything
his brother can achieve.

They are tiny things, these, to set against the mountain of complacency and cynicism and corruption; by themselves they
would surely be overwhelmed by the power that is so vast in the
rest of the book. And it is for this reason that the constancy of
Little Dorrit is so important for Dickens. *Nobody's Fault* would
have been almost a despairing book, reflecting the tone of mind
that one finds in Dickens's letters of the period at which the novel
was begun. As he wrote to Macready (5 October 1854):

> What with teaching people to 'keep in their stations', what with
> bringing up the soul and body of the land to be a good child, or to
> go to the beer-shop, to go a-poaching and go to the devil . . . what
> with flunkyism, toadyism, letting the most contemptible lords come
> in for all manner of places, reading the Court Circular for the New
> Testament, I do reluctantly believe that the English people are
> habitually consenting parties to the miserable imbecility into which
> we have fallen, *and never will help themselves out of it.*

The change of emphasis towards the centre that the book has
now meant a reassertion of Dickens's characteristic hopefulness

and buoyancy of spirit in the creation of a figure who, ignored and misunderstood throughout, is nevertheless, as Professors Butt and Tillotson put it, 'the fount of moral strength, the protectress'. That such a figure should tend to be somewhat unreal is not necessarily a defect in a book which moves so freely to the edge of fantasy. But undoubtedly the burden of moral weight is too great for the pathos of her position to withstand: Dickens in fact confounds the sad loneliness of Little Dorrit's lot with the moral strength she is there to supply, as if the one guaranteed the other and was in fact virtually identical with it; and on occasion he can let himself down very badly:

> Away they went, Little Dorrit turning at the door to say 'God bless you!' She said it very softly, but perhaps she may have been as audible above—who knows!—as a whole cathedral choir.   I, xiv

Who knows indeed? It obviously depends on the cathedral choir. Dickens is so affected by the pathos of it all that he introduces a totally alien and unjustified comparison, puts on a solemn hushed voice (the hush including a refusal properly to commit himself to what he is saying—'perhaps', 'who knows!') and in so doing devalues whatever affecting simplicity the scene might have had: he has obtruded an external *literary* effect on to what must be a natural gesture if it is to be worth anything; and the result is an insult to any dignity Little Dorrit may have attained. The change from *Nobody's Fault* to *Little Dorrit* is a remarkable tribute to the toughness and resilience of Dickens's spirit in the dark times of 1854 and '55, but it is not in Little Dorrit herself that the supreme qualities of the book lie.

(iv) 'GREAT EXPECTATIONS'

Great Expectations is, with *Hard Times,* Dickens's best-plotted novel. In saying this I do not mean simply that the story is plausible and interesting and consistent and without distracting irrelevancies. If we notice the absence of irrelevancies we must be aware of a central interest or theme in terms of which relevance can be defined. The theme of a novel may also cautiously be likened to its central purpose, though in using this word it is as well for us to remember Lawrence's warning of the danger of nailing a novel down to an ulterior motive in the writer. Thus the theme of *The Pilgrim's Progress* can be shortly defined as the way of salvation, and its purpose to persuade men along that road. *Pilgrim's Progress* is hardly a novel in the ordinary sense, and it is its special allegorical character which enables us to pick out its 'purpose' with confidence. But if we look for example at *Emma,* I think we can say without serious distortion that Jane Austen's main interest and concern through the novel, to which her observation of social manners is ancillary and subordinate, is the growth of conscience and moral understanding. And the theme of *Hard Times* is what happens, to the individual and to his environment, when one becomes possessed by a philosophy or pseudo-philosophy which dominates and cramps one's whole being.

A novel is well plotted when, as well as having the elementary virtues of interest, plausibility, economy and consistency, the plot appears to be a natural vehicle for the working out of the theme, so that the theme seems to grow spontaneously out of the narrative of events. One then sees that the theme is simply a crystallisation of a way of looking at that certain selected section of life which forms the narrative. The excellence of *Great Expectations* in this respect can be seen by comparing it with *Martin Chuzzlewit* and *David Copperfield,* two earlier novels with which it has interesting connexions.

The theme of *Martin Chuzzlewit* is self-centredness and its power to delude and to cloud reality (obviously close to the heart of *Great Expectations* too): the force of this can be felt, positively or negatively, in almost every character in the book, and it is formally announced by Old Martin as his main preoccupation. The great strength of *Martin Chuzzlewit* lies in the apparently inexhaustible energy of its satirical observation, and it is a tribute to this that it can make connexions of some kind between so many disparate elements with little obvious strain, that the reader is so carried along in the current of this energy as to overlook a good deal of arbitrariness in the construction of the story and inconsistency of narrative technique. So loose are the links between some of the members of the great caravanserai moving through the pages that at times the various story-lines appear to be there simply as illustrations of Dickens's chosen theme. Martin's suddenly taking off for America, though acceptable as an instance of his flightiness, is obviously motivated by Dickens's desire to have a go at the United States (and at the same time bring in some representatives of a kind of self-absorption too gross to be plausible in England). Nor is Martin's illness, which is the occasion and the part cause of his learning a new humility, a natural growth out of his self-made smallness of mind: its effect on him, as for the first time in his life he becomes utterly dependent on another and can no longer keep up a pretence to himself of superior claims or abilities, is perfectly plausible, though we are rather told of the change than actually shown it happening; but the event itself is, as it were, deliberately injected by Dickens from outside. (And we may note how gruesomely real, by contrast, is Rogue Riderhood's escape from drowning in *Our Mutual Friend*, xxxvi.) I shall try to show that the climax of events which brings Pip to a crisis of self-knowledge is greatly more powerful because it is self-engendered. Moreover, because Dickens's target in *Martin Chuzzlewit* is so wide, and because he wants to use Martin as his great example of regeneration (as contrasted with the unregenerable Pecksniff) he must use different techniques in portraying them: Martin must be seen partly from inside, Pecksniff cannot be; and this produces of course a sense that different characters are getting different treatment for special and ulterior reasons, which in effect prejudge the issue of the story. This approach results in 'good' characters of a vacuous solemnity extreme even for Dickens: almost any paragraph dealing with Tom Pinch is designed to work on the reader a sense of his complete simplicity, humility, unawareness of any claims he as a person ought to have on anyone else; and the result is (what Dickens is very far from intending) that he is both quite unreal and very dull, a stupid and unrewarding companion, and in short a bore.

Contrast in *Great Expectations* the treatment of Biddy, who is one of the unacknowledged keepers of Pip's conscience, but whose simplicity and goodness are entirely convincing and exceptionally impressive as positive merits of her own. Here is Pip 'regretting' his gentlemanly aspirations and wishing he still loved the life at the forge:

> 'If I could have settled down and been but half as fond of the forge as I was when I was little, I know it would have been much better for me. You and I and Joe would have wanted nothing then, and Joe and I would perhaps have gone partners when I was out of my time, and I might even have grown up to keep company with you, and we might have sat on this very bank on a fine Sunday, quite different people. I should have been good enough for *you*; shouldn't I, Biddy?'
>
> Biddy sighed as she looked at the ships sailing on, and returned for answer, 'Yes; I am not over-particular.' It scarcely sounded flattering, but I knew she meant well. GE xvii

Not only are Pip's naïve complacency and sense of his own status and deserts shown up here with a directness and piquancy beyond anything in the earlier novel; but Biddy's reply comprehends a personal dignity and wisdom which are an answer to Pip's conceit impossible in a Tom Pinch. *He* never thinks anything less than he merits or might achieve. *She* knows that her horizon must be limited and ('not being over-particular') will find happiness within her own world; but her sigh towards the ships which imply a world beyond hers suggests with great delicacy her sense of how much is and must remain out of her reach. And unlike Mark Tapley who preserves a respect for Martin Chuzzlewit at his worst, Biddy sees Pip exactly as he is: she can do this because Dickens does not expect Pip to grow into a hero of commanding moral authority. So here he can expose Pip's silly vanity with a clarity which in no way threatens to conflict with Pip's moral growth: how that last phrase just quoted reveals the depth of his ignorance! how little he knows in comparison with Biddy!

In *Martin Chuzzlewit*, therefore, it seems to me that Dickens, attempting to combine satirical and realistic modes of narration, requires a double attitude in the reader which is hard to sustain and which overstrains his moral credulity. *David Copperfield* is in one respect a more centrally organised book, in that it is written in the first person and tells (directly) only the narrator's experiences. At the same time, being told by the hero, it purports to

174

register (directly) only the hero's opinions and attitudes. Yet we hardly need Dickens's self-confessed partiality for this novel, or his introduction of autobiographical elements within it, to confirm our sense that David is in league with his author. As a child, until he reaches Dover and finds sympathy and affluence at one go, he is always an object of pity simply because he is so ill-used, and so we are pretty well bound to be on his side. When he is grown up we know that he behaves foolishly, and his admission of this is amusingly told:

> I lived primarily on Dora and coffee. In my love-lorn condition, my appetite languished; and I was glad of it, for I felt as though it would have been an act of perfidy towards Dora to have a natural relish for my dinner. DC xxxviii

But David remains essentially the morally reliable centre who feels and expresses the right opinions about Uriah Heep and Annie and Mr. Peggotty and the rest: even his too ready acceptance of Steerforth is insisted on as a good fault, the result of too much love. So in the event David inevitably becomes a prig; and his lack of moral growth means that he himself can be little more than a recorder of things that happen to him (or to others) without deeply affecting him.

The story is presented as if it were the subject of a memoir—David in narrating 'cannot always remember' details: the device is transparent, for we all know that the book is a novel, and the author can 'remember' anything he chooses to. But a genuine memoir almost always consists of a fairly loose string of experiences tied together by the accident of their happening to or coming within the ken of one person. Most human lives have no more than this accidental coherence. Likewise there is no guiding theme to *David Copperfield*, only a bundle of stories in which the narrator is haphazardly involved. Moreover David himself is not interesting enough to keep the reader keenly alert to the effects of his adventures on him: he happens to take a leading part in some of the stories, but his main function is to be the universal moral recorder. This is in any case a tricky part for a first-person narrator to keep up; but the identification of author and narrator leads to further strains. David is not by nature satirically or even ironically given; yet the book contains large-scale satirical portraits which have to be conveyed through him. This does not present any special difficulties in Mr. Micawber's case, for he largely describes himself through his speeches and letters; but with Uriah Heep we are up against something different. He is one of Dickens's most venomous creatures, and the author's dislike is patent. The portrait may well be, even as satire, overdrawn—that is not here at issue. What is to the point is that much of the reader's impression of him is gained not through what he does or says, but through David's description of his appearance and the impression he makes. His writhings are real enough, but it is impossible at times to avoid a feeling of special pleading against him, of Dickens with his knife in Uriah using the sensitive, fair-minded David to force the reader's attitude. It is made a point against him that not only does he pretend to a humility which in truth he does not own, but that he has a coarse accent and drops his aitches—which would be relevant if he also pretended to gentility, but he does not. That suggests snobbery in Dickens as well as in David, which becomes really vicious in the scene in which David is obsessed by Heep's physical repulsiveness (see p. 55).

Great Expectations is the only other Dickens novel told entirely in the first person. But there is also *Bleak House*, with its striking device of alternating two quite different methods of narration—a third-person narrative in the historic present and Esther Summerson's story in the conventional past tense. W. J. Harvey has argued that the admitted insipidity of Esther's character is a small price to pay for the 'clear window, lucid and neutral' through which we are able to look at the 'teeming Dickensian world'. Few readers have found much to delight them in Esther: as Harvey says, 'the exigencies of the narrative force [Dickens] to reveal Esther's goodness in a coy and repellent manner; she is, for instance, continually imputing to others qualities which the author transparently wishes us to transfer to her'. What makes such falseness more damaging is that she is not really neutral like a window: like David Copperfield she is the author's moral mouthpiece. *She* is the person (unlike the adored but impractical Jarndyce) who sees through Skimpole, and who not only sees what is wrong with Mrs. Jellyby and Mr. Turveydrop but knows something of how to cope with the situations they create; she is the one to whom the others instinctively turn. Yet there is almost nothing in Esther herself to give the reader confidence in her as more than an outline recorder of the human scene which she witnesses. Though terrible things happen to her from her conception onwards, she remains inwardly unaffected: we cannot accept the judgments she is given to express as coming out of her experience. Since the clarity of Esther's moral vision is something that Dickens relies on as a medium from the start of the narrative, experience cannot be allowed to mature her through the novel, and hence she cannot herself be truly involved in the dramatic action of the story. Furthermore, because she is so untouched by events, we cannot even completely rely on her as a recorder; we cannot trust her power of selection and emphasis. Percipience is not just a matter of having good eyesight and hearing, for the perception of human affairs involves weighting and evaluation: there is no absolute truth attainable by us, only a view of the truth from a given, necessarily limited position; and the more securely rooted in human experience this position, the greater human value will perception from it have. And lest it should seem that I have been writing as if Esther, and not Dickens, were the real author, I emphasise that it is impossible to see the events she narrates and the characters she describes except through her eyes, so entirely has Dickens identified his attitudes with hers. How do we know what Jarndyce is really like, having only such a partial witness to tell us? The great danger of fixing moral authority in a first-person narrator is that there is no place for the author to make a stand outside him.

Another way of putting this point is to say that Esther's narrative, like David's, is insufficiently dramatised. Plainly in a first-person narrative the only attitudes that can be expressed directly are those of the narrator himself, except of course where dialogue allows others to put forward their own views. It may seem odd to say that the reader can place much more confidence in Pip's narrative than in Esther's, for through much of the book he is disastrously wrong in his interpretation of events and miserably narrow and twisted in his human evaluations, as Esther never is. But we are not obliged to see through Pip's eyes as we are through Esther's. We have no chance to have any view of Jarndyce, say, except hers, because everything we are told about him is coloured by her own impressions; whereas, though we never learn anything of Miss Havisham except what Pip tells us, he never tells us what we are to think of her, and the actions which settle our opinion of her are innocent of interpretative colouring from Pip. She shows what she is directly, by saying and doing things which Pip's report gives—we feel sure—without bias or prejudice. But why do we feel so sure that the report is to be relied on? Essentially, I think, because Pip's vision remains throughout radically innocent, and because there is never any question of Dickens being in league with him. He never attempts to cover up for himself, he exposes himself thoroughly; though his motives are unworthy and his behaviour often deplorable, he is never shifty, he gives the reader every opportunity to make the most sharply critical judgment of him—indeed he often openly invites it. So, in the exchange with Biddy quoted above (p. 174), Pip, blind as he is at the time to moral realities, condemns himself out of his own mouth. Such honesty cannot be feigned, and so we believe him for the rest also, all the more because Pip so unflinchingly displays the extent to which he was self-deceived, and because the process of the book *is* the movement in him from moral blindness and confusion to the bleak, melancholy clarity of the end. It is plain that Dickens is morally detached from Pip: his is the objective eye, and only at the end, and in retrospect, is this identified with the view of the narrator.

So the narrative technique of a first-person novel is closely bound up with the human percipience of the hero: what can be told or shown depends on the qualities the author sees in him. *David Copperfield* is—at any rate for the adult reader—rather a dull book, not because exciting or interesting adventures do not happen to or near the hero but because they have so small an effect on him. He is morally invulnerable, and therefore his range of perception is small: it is no accident that the moral attitudes of the book (which are essentially those of David himself) are conventional and stereotyped; there is no way in the book in which judgments of another kind could be expressed.

By contrast, the excellence of the general design of *Great Expectations* lies in the accuracy with which the plot registers the steady development of the central theme—the growth from moral ignorance to wisdom, which in a true first-person narrative must be a matter of *self*-discovery. Growth of this kind happens elsewhere in Dickens of course—in Mr. Dombey, in Eugene Wrayburn, above all in Mr. Gradgrind—and I have suggested above that Martin Chuzzlewit undergoes an enlightenment which is a kind of parody of Pip's, but that in this case Dickens has to provide a totally external stimulus to bring it off. It is one aspect of Dickens's consummate mastery in *Great Expectations* that, without any strain on our credulity, without our feeling it at all strange that Pip should believe it all, the whole edifice of his imaginary world, with all its teasingness and deception, is shown to be essentially his own creation. It is because the deception is a self-deception that the discovery of the truth is so painful, so moving, and so complete: after such knowledge discovered in such a way, the world can have no more terrors. It is true of course that Pip has bad luck, that things are against him; that Miss Havisham and Jaggers deliberately do not undeceive him when they could; that Estella first gives him the idea, that he is coarse and common and so inspires him with his desire for a false gentility. The world in which he moves conspires with his deceiving self. Yet what is so strong throughout the book is the sense of Pip's making his own heedless career out of the opportunities put in his way. His certainty that what he aspires to is not only worthy but also his destiny leads him to feel that the world must be on his side and waiting for him: but the world at which he has set his sights is in fact quite indifferent to him. As Jaggers says, there was 'not a particle of evidence' for Pip's notion that Miss Havisham was his benefactress: what Pip primarily relied on was not the seeming acquiescence of Miss Havisham herself but his sense that gentility and union with Estella were his by right and made him morally superior to Joe and Biddy and the life he left behind him. Everything that points to his construction of his own future being no more than a house of cards he rejects or turns into evidence against himself. Pip himself has a word for it:

It was clear that I must repair to our town next day, and in the first flow of my repentance it was equally clear that I must stay at Joe's. But, when I had secured my box-place by tomorrow's coach, and had been down to Mr. Pocket's and back, I was not by any means convinced on the last point, and began to invent reasons and make excuses for putting up at the Blue Boar. I should be an inconvenience at Joe's; I was not expected, and my bed would not be ready; I should be too far from Miss Havisham's, and she was exacting and mightn't like it. All other swindlers upon earth are nothing to the self-swindlers, and with such pretences did I cheat myself. Surely a curious thing. That I should innocently take a bad half-crown of somebody else's manufacture, is reasonable enough; but that I should knowingly reckon the spurious coin of my own make as good money! An obliging stranger, under pretence of compactly folding up my bank-notes for security's sake, abstracts the notes and gives me nutshells; but what is his sleight of hand to mine, when I fold up my own nutshells and pass them on myself as notes! xxviii

There must be few readers hard-boiled enough to be able to resist wincing at so merciless an exposure of so intimate and familiar a kind of self-deceit.

That passage is in a vein of detached meditation most unusual in Dickens and suggestive for a moment of George Eliot. But as a whole *Great Expectations* impresses itself as certainly the most psychological of Dickens's novels, and my account assumes that this impression is essentially a true one. Yet it is still very much a Dickens novel; the working out of the story has the form of a gigantic fable with the immense symbolic figures of Magwitch and Miss Havisham presiding over the whole like choric puppet-masters. On a smaller scale Mrs. Pocket and Mrs. Gargery are quite as amazing as anything in *Little Dorrit*. Wemmick's life and the part he plays in the story are fantastic, with a bizarre logic which yet in a ghoulish way fits on to Pip's real experience. The fable and all its inmates form the schema within which Pip slowly and painfully learns the truth about his own real life. Only, whereas the fable of *Little Dorrit* directly, if fantastically, reflects the real world, it is Pip who is himself responsible for creating the deceptive interpretation of the fabulous schema for which he falls so completely, passing on his own nutshells.

It is because his dream world has been so much his own creation and its collapse ultimately his responsibility alone that Pip's humiliation is so deep. Most of us feel an impulse to blame others when things go wrong; but Pip has no one to blame. It is worse even than Nobody's Fault, it is his own fault. The humiliation comes in the most shocking and brutal way; yet Magwitch's part in it is entirely innocent. For he knew nothing of Miss Havisham and Estella, and how could *he* see that Pip would feel himself corrupted by his money? I am sure that it is important to understand that Pip's violent reaction to Magwitch, his horror at the convict's physical presence, is really motivated by the crash of his dreams, not by any essential viciousness remaining in Magwitch himself. When Pip asks whether there were no one else responsible for providing the money,

> 'No,' said he, with a glance of surprise: 'who else should there be? And, dear boy, how good-looking you have growed! There's bright eyes somewheres—eh? Isn't there bright eyes somewheres, wot you love the thoughts on?'
> Estella, Estella!   xxxix

So Estella is the central motive of all, though Pip's yearning for her cannot be separated from his yearning to be a 'gentleman': it was Estella who first gave Pip his notions of gentility, who made him aspire beyond his own world, for whom he deserted and despised those who truly loved him. His abhorrence of Magwitch comes from the sudden revelation that the world he has constructed is built on sand; and his instinctive reaction is to shudder at and stand off from the man who has innocently provided him with the grounds for deceiving himself, and now equally innocently causes him to face the truth. He feels thus that he has been corrupted, he has touched pitch, and for worse than nothing: he has not been raised from his old life, he has sunk below it; and after all, the spring of his desire for wealth and finery is a chimera of his own brain. (Christopher Ricks notes (*Dickens and the Twentieth Century*, p. 200) how the little episode of Magwitch's burning the two 'clean and new notes' which Pip proffered brilliantly and unobtrusively symbolises the end of Pip's corrupt idea that there is some crucial moral difference between clean money—the gentlemanly fortune he thought he had from Miss Havisham—and dirty—the 'two fat sweltering one-pound notes that seemed to have been on terms of the warmest intimacy with all the cattle markets in the county'—by making him realise on what his gentlemanliness is based.)

So what happens at this stage in Pip's fortunes is a sudden humiliation, the implications of which for his own moral life he tries to shield himself from in a sense of horror at the agent of it:

> He ate in a ravenous way that was very disagreeable, and all his actions were uncouth, noisy and greedy. Some of his teeth had failed him since I saw him eat on the marshes, and as he turned his food in his mouth, and turned his head sideways to bring his strongest fangs to bear upon it, he looked terribly like a hungry old dog.
>
> If I had begun with any appetite, he would have taken it away, and I should have sat much as I did—repelled from him by an insurmountable aversion, and gloomily looking at the cloth.   xl

This is somewhat reminiscent of David's view of Uriah Heep, but there is a vital difference in the functions of the two passages. In the earlier case we are supposed to be seeing the true Uriah Heep and judging him; in this one our sense is strong that Pip's vision has become distorted by his sickening knowledge of the significance Magwitch has for him, and so we are concerned with it as a mark against Pip: he will not see the plain man, only his coarseness and ungentlemanly manners. Of course it is true that Pip the young gentleman has been created by Magwitch as his revenge on society, just as Estella the heartless is created by Miss Havisham as hers: if Magwitch cannot become a gentleman himself he will make one. So Pip has perhaps some small right to feel ill-used. Yet something, I believe, goes wrong with this group of scenes. Herbert too feels an aversion to Magwitch which takes the petty form of his starting up from a chair in which Magwitch had sat, as if it were polluted. Professor Ricks argues that by this device Dickens ensures that Pip's immediate repugnance is saved from being disgusting: Herbert is 'simple, unsnobbish and good-natured' and so his reaction is to be relied on as giving the truth about Magwitch. But the truth is quite visible in other ways; and Dickens's trick is on the contrary unsatisfactory just because Magwitch shows himself to be rough and coarse but not deeply repellent in himself. Herbert's gesture is not guaranteed, proved sound by his good nature: it just seems out of character, and his concurrence in Pip's mood gives a specious objectivity to the reaction that the whole situation shows to be unjustified. For the main point must be that Magwitch's 'offence' is to have been the unwitting occasion of Pip's erecting a grand edifice of ideas about and around himself. Pip's self-reproach—and this Dickens gives with great accuracy of psychological observation—instinctively vents itself first as abhorrence of the innocent cause of his new agony. At the crash of his world Pip is still the snobbish self-regarding person he has been for so long, though now a somewhat chastened one. For this Herbert must be the sympathetic and discerning friend to his distress, not the accomplice of his egoism. Nevertheless his love for Herbert (a love which came comparatively easily, for Herbert is a part of Pip's new genteel world, but which is still disinterested love, the first real sign of regeneration in him)—this love makes him humble himself before Miss Havisham and learn by this act that he has in fact nothing to forgive her for. Such self-discovery is always intensely painful, and in Pip's case all the more so because it must be accomplished by something like public confession of his folly and ignorance.

But Pip's final repudiation of his old self is the love which in the end he comes to feel for Magwitch, a love all the clearer for having come to replace repulsion and abhorrence. The falsenesses he has erected about himself are all knocked down, and as he clears away the rubble of his ruined dream world, Pip sees, one after another, the truths he has so long ignored or denied. The last truth is to recognise in Magwitch the suffering human being, to see him as a man, not classified or categorised as criminal or vulgarian. Snobbery is the categorisation and evaluation of men by artificial distinctions. So now Pip's clear-sighted love is the end of all his snobbery:

> now my repugnance to him had all melted away, and in the hunted, wounded, shackled creature who held my hand in his, I only saw a man who had meant to be my benefactor, and who had felt affectionately, gratefully, and generously, towards me with great constancy through a series of years. I only saw in him a much better man than I had been to Joe.   liv

It is a transition over an immense moral distance, from complete self-absorption to a self-negation which sees only the object of love and is heroic only in the degree of self-denial involved. In its context the change is completely convincing. How is this managed? Entirely, I think, by the subtlest manipulation of the narrative technique. From the point (in Chapter xliv) when Pip returns from seeing Miss Havisham for the last time but one, when, that is, Magwitch's danger has become apparent, the interest—*his* interest in relating what happens—gradually shifts from himself to Magwitch (his action in saving Miss Havisham from the fire is instinctive and utterly unself-regarding and unself-conscious, as we see from his being unaware so long of the injury to his hands), from then till the superb Chapter liv, the description of the flight down river and Magwitch's capture, we are aware of Pip only as a part of the action and the recorder of what he sees. Or rather, he serves as the medium through which attention is directed to Magwitch: we are aware not of Pip so much as of Magwitch as the centre of Pip's concern. How vivid and fresh the river scene is—because Pip sees it through clear eyes and with his attention all on one outward object which makes sharp perception so urgent a necessity. Note, as one small instance, the conversation with the jack about the galley, so unobtrusive but so telling as each word eats into Pip on Magwitch's account. What therefore is happening in this wonderful chapter is that the narrative act is itself an enactment of the main issue that it relates. As love means ceasing to care for oneself, so the narrative shifts the attention from Pip to the object of his love. Throughout the book, of course, the narrator is Pip as he has been made wise by suffering: so his view is always retrospective; yet the telling of the story is so designed as to reveal at each moment the vision of the boy and young man as he was then. There is thus no moral parading of the young Pip by his older and wiser self: the absurdities are left to speak for themselves, and Pip's developing nature is directly revealed simply in the honest telling of what happens to him and how he thinks about it.

In a discussion laying stress on how admirably the plotting of *Great Expectations* is designed in relation to its gradually expanding and suddenly contracting theme, it would be disingenuous to say nothing of the coincidences on which the resolution of the story depends. Considered in the abstract they are as fantastic as anything in *Oliver Twist*. Do not such departures from plausibility, from 'what happens in real life', detract from a story so much of the virtue of which is in its emotional realism? Certainly, though they are a part with the structure of the fable whose importance has already been stressed, they do detract, especially for their very late introduction where, as Ricks says, 'it is easy to feel that they exist not, legitimately, as a means to writing the novel, but illegitimately, as a means to rounding it off'. Yet on the one hand how well they *are* introduced—Herbert's simple writing down of the first (Compeyson's link with both Magwitch and Miss Havisham), which is accepted by them both as just a strange fact, Pip's sense of amazement as he realises and prepares Herbert for the second (Magwitch's relation to Estella), paralleling the reader's surprise. And do they, on reflexion, really matter very much at all? They are mechanical devices—slightly strained ones, admittedly—and do not get in the way of the psychological truth of Pip's own story. They might be said to be there only to provide a mystery and also a not very necessary neatness of the kind of which Dickens was so fond.

Nothing essential to the greatness of *Great Expectations* is lost by discounting them altogether. (And there is of course a sardonic aptness for Pip's story that in taking Magwitch's money he was, unknown to all, getting as close as he ever gets to Estella.)

The coincidence of Jaggers being both Miss Havisham's and Magwitch's lawyer is of course crucial, but it is not really implausible in itself (there is only a limited number of lawyers anyway); and when the truth comes out, it simply strikes one as one of the bits of bad luck which conspire with Pip's own inclinations to deceive him. Jaggers is a major factor in the book's overall success. Not only is he an essential part of the construction of the plot; he has a very important symbolic function as well. The law, which in earlier Dickens has been a monstrous contraption of mismanagement, obstruction and inaction, is here personified in Jaggers as the dehumaniser of all human relationships. For him truth is only what can be established at law; and the evidence of what the law can do is what it has done. So he keeps the two hideous heads in his office and Estella's mother for his servant, as signs of his own power over the truth: he despises those whom he lives off, showing his contempt in the ritual handwashing with which he gets rid of each client. Likewise he despises Joe's disinterestedness and is angry with Pip for refusing anything from Miss Havisham at the end. Jaggers's forensic skill has corrupted his life to the point where right and wrong, truth and falsehood, only exist so far as they can be proven at law (he exults especially in having bought off Magwitch against the weight of evidence and against what he knows to be the truth). His law represents the denial or elimination of all natural human impulse: he contrives to draw out and make palpable what evil can be found, though without clarity or openness of motive.

So Jaggers's state is the opposite of Pip's. It is in the sense that Jaggers is, according to this account, fundamentally corrupted that I have called Pip fundamentally innocent. Grossly though Pip deceives himself, he does not wilfully deny or manipulate the truth (and nor even does Miss Havisham); Jaggers, on the other hand, never allows himself to go beyond the evidence, never admits anything; yet his whole career is a falsification of essential human truth. At one point (Chapter li), where he makes Pip see the pointlessness of telling Estella about her father, there is a sign as of a curtain lifted, and Jaggers appears for a moment with human sensibilities; but only for a moment, and the curtain comes down again all the more brusquely and firmly immediately afterwards. Wemmick's is a transitional, or better a divided, case: he can only keep his humanity alive where it is most needed by the most rigid separation of his home life from his work at the office. In the office, and when he is with Jaggers, he is a mere legal machine, and it always takes him time to 'unscrew' himself from the effects of being with his employer. Moreover, the anti-humane standards by which Jaggers and the office function, colour even Wemmick's private life. He lives according to the gospel of personal property, symbolically securing his own (which includes Miss Skiffins and the Aged) in the grotesque little castle in Walworth; his conversation, even at home, is never naturally open or unguarded. The proof of Pip's essential innocence is his extreme vulnerability; Jaggers represents the total opposite of this, and even Wemmick only becomes vulnerable when for a moment Pip breaks the rules and brings Walworth into the office in his desperate appeal that human feelings should not be kept out of account altogether.

Finally a word about the two endings. The 20th century has on the whole had little patience with the softer ending which Dickens wrote after Edward Bulwer Lytton had urged him against the quiet melancholy with which, in the first version, he leaves Estella and Pip separate. Monroe Engel has argued (*The Maturity of Dickens*, p. 166) that once Estella has been recognised as Magwitch's true daughter—and so presumably touched with commonness and even criminality—it is proper that she and Pip should come together. But this is part of the somewhat contrived side of the novel, which insists on rounding off the story with melodramatic mystery and coincidence, the aspect where—it is the only instance in *Great Expectations*—Dickens allows psychological truth to be twisted a bit by the demands of an external symbolic structure. This is not

187

something giving strength to the book; and surely a relaxed, warm conclusion, in the tranquil, but clearly secure, calm of evening, spoils the effect of Pip's final moment of truth when he discovers that he has lost not only Estella but also Biddy and the chance of quiet happiness back on the marshes. That he might still, after all the disasters, marry Biddy is his final piece of romancing: the wistful irony of it lies in its having at one time (when his for the asking) counted for so little with him, while now it represents for a moment all he can desire, yet even then sometimes eternally beyond his reach and the pathos of this is certainly much reduced if a small renunciation, however overwhelming at the time, is to be rewarded at the end by something so much greater. In truth perhaps the matter of the eventual ending is of small account; for Pip's story really ends when he knows everything about himself, and that is at the end not of the last chapter but of the last but one. But since, properly, we could not be left with nothing whatever of Estella after her marriage, I am sure that Edmund Wilson is right in calling Dickens's original close 'perfect in tone and touch'. What happiness Pip and Estella can now find comes not from any kind of fortune outside either one of them, but simply from the possession of the wisdom of real experience deeply felt; and for this Dickens's first instinct, as he continued to look the hard truth calmly but directly in the face, seems to me to have been unquestionably right:

> I was very glad afterwards to have had the interview; for, in her face and in her voice, and in her touch, she gave me the assurance that suffering had been stronger than Miss Havisham's teaching, and had given her a heart to understand what my heart used to be.
>
> l, original version

Bibliography

At the end of *The Dickens Critics* George Ford and Lauriat Lane print a bibliography, which is, as they say, 'a selection from the impossibly enormous body of material written about Dickens and the fiction of Dickens before 1960'. It is nevertheless twenty-four pages long. My list therefore can be no more than a very brief personal selection of books and articles which I have found useful or interesting, and which are fairly easy to get hold of. A medium-length list is included in Christopher Hibbert's *The Making of Charles Dickens*.

TEXTS

There are innumerable editions of the novels, some of which (e.g. the Oxford Illustrated Dickens) reprint the original illustrations by Phiz and others. A new critical edition of the novels has begun to come out under the editorship of Kathleen Tillotson. So far only *Oliver Twist* has appeared (Oxford University Press). Sets of *Household Words* and *All the Year Round* can still sometimes be found in second-hand shops. Dickens's own contributions to *Household Words* have lately been collected in an edition by Harry Stone (Allen Lane: the Penguin Press). The Nonesuch edition of the *Letters* (1938) is very far from complete. A new complete edition, by Madeline House and Graham Storey (Clarendon Press), has been begun. The *Speeches* were edited by K. J. Fielding (Oxford University Press, 1960).

BACKGROUND

Buckley, J. H.: *The Victorian Temper* (Vintage paperback, 1964).

Cruikshank, R. J.: *Charles Dickens and Early Victorian England* (Pitman, 1949). Well illustrated from contemporary prints, etc.

Houghton, W. E.: *The Victorian Frame of Mind* (Yale University Press, 1957).

Kitson Clark, G.: *The Making of Victorian England* (Methuen, 1962).

Trollope, T. A.: *What I Remember* (1887).

Young, G. M. (ed.): *Early Victorian England* (Oxford University Press, 1934). A very valuable and well illustrated survey.

DICKENS'S LIFE

John Forster's *Life of Charles Dickens* was much criticised when first published and has now been to some extent superseded. But it will always be important for its copious first-hand material. It is available in Everyman's Library and elsewhere. The most comprehensive biography is Edgar Johnson's *Charles Dickens, His Tragedy and Triumph* (2 vols., Gollancz, 1953). Christopher Hibbert's *The Making of Charles Dickens* is an extremely worthwhile account of Dickens's earlier life in relation to his life's work. Of special interest are the *Memories of My Father* and *Recollections* (1929 and 1934) by Henry Fielding Dickens, and Gladys Storey's *Dickens and Daughter* (1939), based on conversations with Kate Dickens (Mrs. Pellegrini).

CRITICAL AND OTHER STUDIES

Butt, John and Tillotson, Kathleen: *Dickens at Work* (Methuen, 1957). A most interesting study of the actual writing of the novels, taken from Dickens's notebooks, letters, etc.

Daleski, H. M: *Dickens and the Art of Analogy* (Faber and Faber, 1970).

Ford, George: *Dickens and his Readers* (Princeton University Press, 1955). A study of Dickens's changing reputation.

Ford, George and Lane, Lauriat (eds.): *The Dickens Critics* (Cornell University Press, 1961). A selection of essays from 1841 to 1960.

Garis, Robert: *The Dickens Theatre: A Reassessment of the Novels* (Clarendon Press, 1965).

Gissing, George: *Charles Dickens* (1898).

Gross, John and Pearson, Gabriel (eds.): *Dickens and the Twentieth Century* (Routledge and Kegan Paul, 1962). Essays by various hands.

House, Humphry: *The Dickens World* (Oxford University Press, 1941).

House, Humphry: *All in Due Time* (Hart-Davis, 1955).

Leavis, F. R.: *The Great Tradition* (Chatto and Windus, 1948).

Leavis, F. R. and Q. D.: *Dickens the Novelist* (Chatto and Windus, 1970).

Orwell, George: 'Charles Dickens' (in *Inside the Whale*, Penguin, 1940).

Tillotson, Kathleen: *Novels of the* 1840s (Oxford University Press, 1954).

Wilson, Edmund: 'Dickens: The Two Scrooges' (in *The Wound and the Bow*, Methuen, 1941).

Index of Dickens's Works

The main references are in heavy type